AMERICAN MADONNA

* * * * * * * * * * *

AMERICAN MADONNA

* * * * * * * * * * * * * * *

Crossing Borders with the Virgin Mary

Deirdre Cornell

ORBIS BOOKS

Maryknoll, New York 10545

Founded in 1970, Orbis Books endeavors to publish works that enlighten the mind, nourish the spirit, and challenge the conscience. The publishing arm of the Maryknoll Fathers & Brothers, Orbis seeks to explore the global dimensions of the Christian faith and mission, to invite dialogue with diverse cultures and religious traditions, and to serve the cause of reconciliation and peace. The books published reflect the views of their authors and do not represent the official position of the Maryknoll Society. To learn more about Maryknoll and Orbis Books, please visit our website at www.maryknollsociety.org.

Library of Congress Cataloging-in-Publication Data

Cornell, Deirdre.
 American Madonna : crossing borders with the Virgin Mary / Deirdre Cornell.
   p. cm.
 ISBN 978-1-57075-871-3 (pbk.)
 1. Mary, Blessed Virgin, Saint—Devotion to—Mexio—Oaxaca (State) 2. Oaxaca (Mexico : State)—Religious life and customs. 3. Cornell, Deirdre. I. Title.
 BT652.M4C65 2010
 232.910972'74—dc22
                                                                          2010010998

For

José Tomás Bobadilla Acosta

"[V]e al palacio del obispo...y le dirás...lo que mucho deseo, que aquí...me edifique un templo...para en él mostrar y dar todo mi amor, compasión, auxilio y defensa...Mira que ya hayas oído mi mandato, hijo mío el más pequeño; anda y pon todo tu esfuerzo."

"Go to the bishop's palace...and tell him...
that I greatly desire that here...a church be built...
where I can reveal...and give
all my love, compassion, help, and defense...
See to it that you hear my mandate, my dear little son;
go and put forth all your effort."

–Nican Mopohua

and in loving memory of

Sally Cunneen

whose passionate search for Mary, the woman and the symbol, charted my own exploration of "the sea that no one exhausts"

A view of the Soledad Basilica in Oaxaca, Mexico

CONTENTS

ACKNOWLEDGMENTS

I received much help in writing this book.

My maternal grandmother, Carlotta Durkin Ribar, perpetually sought the *Stella Maris* with her otherworldly gaze. On the other end of the spectrum, my five children anchor me to the earthly joys and challenges of being a mother.

With their lifelong commitment to the vision of the Catholic Worker Movement, my parents, Tom and Monica Cornell, my brother, T. Christopher Cornell, and my husband, Kenney Gould, remind me to put faith into practice. My husband gave me feedback for this book on topics historical, psychological, theological, and sociological. Since he shared the pilgrimages and pastoral projects at the heart of this work, his collaboration has been essential.

As a non-Latino writing about Mexican virgins, I owe many debts of hospitality.

Rosaurora Espinoza and other members of the Mexican Grail Movement (including the late and much-missed Isabel Hernández and Licha Kraemer) sponsored an immersion program in which I participated in 1989. Exchanges through the Grail Women of the Americas have been key experiences in my understanding of Latino and Latin American religious practices.

Alicia Butkiewicz and the Maryknoll Lay Missioners made possible the three years that my husband, children, and I spent in Oaxaca.

In that city, my first expression of gratitude belongs to the base ecclesial communities. Sabina and Otilio Hernández Hernández and Efigenia Hernández Martinez received me into their ministry in San Martín Mexicapam.

Our twins' godparents, Ariel Sánchez Hernández and Janeth Lopez Peña, and Teresa Wolff and Gustavo Barón, opened their homes and hearts to us in so many ways.

In the villages of Guadalupe, La Cienaga, and Roaló, the López Olmedo family, the Castellanos Cruz family, and the Aquino López family, respectively, welcomed us to their migrant-sending communities.

Fr. Fernando Cruz Montes's extensive knowledge of local ecclesial history contributed much to my research.

A handful of the few university students from Juquila in the capital happened to reside in our apartment complex. In another coincidence, the grandfather of my daughter's best friend Eliza was a major benefactor of the sanctuary. I am grateful to Juquileños and pilgrims alike who shared testimonies and oral histories.

Two slim volumes that chronicle the history of the Virgin of Juquila and the Virgin of Soledad, the former by Juan Castro Méndez and the latter by Everardo Ramírez Bohórquez, proved to be invaluable resources. The resources in the Santo Domingo Cultural Center, the Burgoa Library, the Museum of the Basilica of the Virgin of Soledad, and the archives room of the Central Public Library of Oaxaca were helpful in furthering my knowledge of the two Oaxacan virgins. Photographs of colonial-era sketches are used with permission of the Francisco de Burgoa Library of the Benito Juarez Autonomous University of Oaxaca, which reserves the rights to their reproduction.

My interpretation of the social conflict in Oaxaca is shaped by contact with the civil associations Flor y Canto, Services for Alternative Education, the 25th of November Committee and with the Archdiocesan Office of Justice and Peace.

Xavier Castellanos Cruz provided research assistance; Zenon Ramírez Montes allowed me to include photos belonging to Distribuidora Lumy; Phil and Kathy Dahl-Bredine made available statistics on free trade; Randy and Susan Hinthorn facilitated my interest in Oaxacan church history; and Mary and Pat Denevan kindly took photos for this work.

Our trips to the Mixteca in Puebla and the Sierra in Querétaro greatly enhanced my understanding of emigration and *Guadalupanismo*. In Puebla, in La Noria Hidalgo we were hosted by the Giron Quiñones family; in Tehuixtla by the Guerrero Fernández family; in Santa Inez Ahuatempan by the Vidal Guevara family; in San Juan Ixcaquixtla by the Ramos Castillo family; in Izúcar de Matamoros by the Rosales Romero family; and in La Magdalena by the Lezama Palma family. From Tehuitzingo, Juan Pérez's website *pueblomixteco* makes a vital connection between sending and migrant communities.

In Querétaro, we were hosted by the Camacho Moran family in Portezuelo and Tequisquiapam; by the Ramírez Fernández family in San Pedro Escanela; by the Ledesma Martínez family in San Joaquín; and by the Moran Trejo family in El Chilar.

In New York, the staff and parishioners of St. Patrick's Church in Newburgh, under pastors Monsignor John Budwick and Father Fernando Hernandez, deserve gratitude for accepting our family into the Spanish-speaking congregation.

Pablo Cruz Guevara brought the *Carrera Antorcha Guadalupana* to Newburgh.

Father Tomás Bobadilla, Brother Dan Crimmins, CFC (of "the *Irish* Christian Brothers"), Sr. Martha Hernandez, OLC, and Sr. María Estrada, OLC, helped guide a pastoral project for immigrants, the *Misión Guadalupana*, described in chapter 3. While other *guadalupanos* of faith and fervor are too many to name, I would be remiss in not acknowledging Daniel Olivo, José "Caco" Guerrero, Pilar Herrera, Lucia Marín, Cayetana Gutierrez, Felix Serru, Mercedes and Esteban Guerrero, Elsa Carrera, Fray José McCarthy, Rosalía Rosales, Fidelina and Fernando Herrera, and Guadalupe and Alfredo Mazarriego.

When translating prayers and songs, I have rendered (to the best of my ability) the poetry and fervor of the original texts. In most cases, I have abridged the hymns selected for this work.

My undergraduate advisor at Smith College, Frederique A. Marglin, inspired me to take another look at the Virgin Mary; Rosemary Curran and Elizabeth Carr served as my role models. At the Jesuit School of Theology at Berkeley, Gloria Loya, PBVM, urged me to look for the Virgin of Guadalupe beyond the sixteenth century; Anne Brotherton, SFCC, directed my thesis work; and Alejandro Garcia-Rivera introduced me to the concept of subaltern religion. Cay Charles, of the Grail in Cornwall, New York, sees to it that in the midst of my other commitments I remain engaged in theological reflection. David Aquije, of *Revista Maryknoll*, graciously reviewed portions of this manuscript.

Mike Leach of Orbis Books took on this project and even gave it a name, coming up with the perfect title; thanks to his unfailing commitment to new Catholic writers, this manuscript found its home at Orbis.

My final and definitive words of gratitude belong to Sally and Joe Cunneen, who accompanied me on the journey of producing this manuscript and provided careful criticism, warm encouragement, and skillful practical advice. Sally died on the eve of All Saints' Day, just as I was finishing this book—a work I would never have undertaken without her. To the end, Sally shared generously the vigorous insightfulness that characterized her as a writer, educator and co-editor, with Joe, of the international ecumenical quarterly *Cross Currents*. Their careers span six decades of helping to shape the faith lives of Christians both within and beyond the borders of the U.S. Catholic Church.

Sally's intelligent devotion to the Virgin Mary demanded from me ever-clearer attempts at articulation. Her veneration of the Mother of God through art taught me to nurture my own relationship with Mary. She and Joe have served for me (and for countless others) as examples of enduring Christian conviction in our contemporary world. May their loving witness and critical faith inspire many more generations to come.

INTRODUCTION

* * * * * * * * *

Every book must start somewhere; this one began in a musty chapel just outside Guadalajara during the last worldwide Eucharistic Congress.

That year, thousands of international participants converged with the millions of Mexican pilgrims who gather annually to celebrate the Virgin of Zapopan's feast day on October 12, *el Día de la Raza*. I flew up from Oaxaca, where my husband and I had just begun a three-year term as foreign missioners. Still attached to my work in the North among immigrants from the South, not yet engaged in the communities they had left behind, I joined the mostly Latino delegation from my area of New York. My own sense of displacement made me acutely aware of the significance of the celebration's date—marking as it does the collision of two worlds—and of its context: Jalisco is one of Mexico's most prominent migrant-sending states.

Visitors streamed into the main church to pay their respects to the *Zapopana*, a saddle virgin (a statue small enough to travel with Spanish soldiers on horseback) brought to Mexico during the Conquest. Eucharistic adoration was taking place in an adjacent smaller church (the original one that predates the enormous temple next door). The *alter ego* of this solemn ceremony, a secular celebration taking place just outside the church's mammoth wooden doors, was a sprawling street fair.

Wary of pickpockets, my companions and I began to elbow our way through the veritable chaos. The entire area had been closed off, but traffic for miles around was still congested. A procession of some twenty men on horseback carried blankets and sleeping mats—they would be spending the night on the square. Sidewalks were choked with booths selling hair accessories, CDs, t-shirts, shoes, religious articles, plastic containers, and other household items. Hawking loudspeakers invited passersby to try their hand at games of chance or skill. People selling traditional foods were standing behind tables laden with regional sweets and next to improvised food stalls. The tantalizing smell of grilled onions and the nutty aroma of fresh-baked bread mingled with the not-so-pleasant odors of the garbage and human waste that lined the gutters.

I was overwhelmed by the size of the plaza and the seeming anarchy there. A huge area in front of the church contained multiple centers of activity. The noise of the street fair was drowned out by a loudspeaker droning prayers in an urgent, disembodied voice that heightened the frenetic atmosphere. Scores of dance troupes, each with its own banner, were performing simultaneously. Dancers' costumes adorned with shells, feathered headdresses, and fringes of small bells gave clear evidence of the Zapopan devotion's indigenous origins; drums and flutes provided the only musical accompaniment. Choreography had to be simple, because the steps would be followed for hours at a time. Not really a performance but more of a ritual, the dancing would go on—day and night—until the feast's cycle ended.

When I entered the small church from the scouring sunlight of the unsheltered plaza, it took some time for my eyes to adjust to the dusk of the enclave. With its richly gilded colonial altarpieces, ornate molding layered with dust, and tile floor grimy from the feet of so many pedestrians, the chapel offered a peaceful, if musty, respite from the chaos outside.

A quick look around the wooden pews revealed that my fellow pilgrims had come from all corners of the globe. Priests, laypeople, and religious in diverse habits knelt before a tiny white disc on the altar, displayed in a magnificent gold monstrance.

Kneeling, I rested in the stillness of eucharistic adoration. The deep silence of the chapel, with its rigid pews and the not-quite-obscured host on the filigreed altar, were somehow essentially connected with the din of the wild, all-too-human street festival outside.

Patronal feasts all over Latin America are held in honor of various saints, of course, but sanctuaries dedicated to the Virgin Mary, in particular, attract pilgrims with impressive efficacy. I wondered as I often have, what is it about the Mother of God that elicits such exuberance? Part of the explanation surely lies in the fact that, as anthropologists Victor and Edith Turner note, for Catholic cultures the Virgin Mary embodies *communitas*: a state of collective mysticism experienced with others, the underlying interconnectedness of any society.

I had experienced this communal fervor before, in celebrations for another beloved Marian representation, Our Lady of Guadalupe. Now, in the drumming and the milling of crowds of pilgrims, the flow of that fervor surged again in my pulse. A verse from John's gospel came to me: "And the bread that I will give for the life of the world is my flesh" (6:51).

This book began in that moment, in my staring at the fragile host on a gilded altar, wondering at these words from John's gospel while taking in the stillness and the commotion together and thinking, *This really* is *the life of the world.*

These words carried meaning for me in another, more personal way: I was newly, unexpectedly pregnant. Tiny twins lay curled like kittens in the hammock of my belly. Thus, giving one's flesh for the life of the world had a literal quality to it, its meaning made more palpably visceral by Mary's offering of her own body.

In the Annunciation—the single most celebrated aspect of Mary's life in scripture and tradition, the crowning pearl of the Marian treasury—a young Jewish girl accepts her vocation and creation is reborn. The Virgin of Zapopan, as a representation of the Mother of God, bears encoded in her miniature image the same collective memory, an annunciation to be enfleshed yet again into history. And it is Mary who has consistently led me—like millions of other women throughout the centuries—to a fuller, deeper, more grounded encounter with Christ: a *gendered* meeting with God.

The two main trajectories that have shaped my life came together at that moment, like two balls tossed from opposite corners in the same direction that grow closer to each other the more they near their destination. The experience of mothering children and the privilege of being radically challenged by the Latin American church joined, for me, in the figure of Mary. A human woman gave birth to Jesus, making God visible; in my own spiritual conjuncture, it was now she, Mary, who became tangible. It is my hope that readers will catch glimpses of her in these pages.

I

Ave Maris Stella
Dei mater alma,
atque semper virgo
felix caeli ponta.

Hail, O Star of the ocean,
God's own Mother blest,
ever sinless Virgin,
gate of heav'nly rest.

Sumens illud Ave
Gabrielis ore
funda nos in pace
mutans Hevae nomen.

Taking that sweet Ave
which from Gabriel came,
peace confirm within us,
changing Eve's name.

Solve vincula reis
profer lumen caecis
mala nostra pelle
bona cuncta posce.

Break the sinners' fetters,
make our blindness day,
Chase all evils from us,
for all blessings pray.

Virgo singularis
inter omnes mites
nos culpis solutos
mites fac et castos.

Virgin all excelling,
mildest of the mild,
free from guilt preserve us
meek and undefiled.

Vitam praesta puram
iter para tutum
ut videntes Iesum
semper collaetemur.

Keep our life all spotless,
make our way secure
till we find in Jesus,
joy for evermore.

MY MOTHER, MY CONFIDENCE

* * * * * * * * * * * * * * * *

Remember, O most gracious Virgin Mary, that never was it known that anyone who fled to your protection, implored your help or sought your intercession was left unaided. Inspired with this confidence, I fly to you, O Virgin of Virgins, my mother. To you I come, before you I stand, sinful and sorrowful. O Mother of the Word Incarnate, despise not my petitions but in your mercy hear and answer me.
— The Memorare

"Cu ix amó nican nicá nimo nantzin?"
"Am I not here, who am your mother?"
— *Nican Mopohua*

No one knows exactly how my grandmother met Our Lady of Guadalupe.

I often wonder how an Irish-American housewife in Ohio became acquainted with this particular image of the Mother of God. Staying up with insomnia as she so often did, did she see shadows darken the ceramic face of the Immaculate Conception statue next to her bed? Did light from the hallway radiate in a sunburst halo caressing the image's back while the rest of the house slept in darkness? However it happened, a lifelong devotion to Our Lady of Guadalupe took my grandmother through time and across continents.

My grandmother nursed a sick father, married, helped start a Catholic Worker house, raised two daughters, and—at fifty years of age—took in four orphaned grandnieces and nephews (the youngest still in diapers). As if to bolster motivation for her myriad maternal duties, she collected holy cards and cluttered her house

3

with fair-haired Madonnas. Entering her middle and later years, however, it was Mary's manifestation as the warm-skinned, Nahu-atl-speaking Virgin that she most treasured. After my grandfather died, she made a pilgrimage to the Basilica of Saint Mary of Guadalupe in Mexico City.

Carrying out a promise to visit her confidante meant entering un-known linguistic, geographic, and cultural territory—a challenge my grandmother met with rare courage. This uncharacteristic willingness to traverse boundaries in her old age surprised everyone who knew her. She rarely traveled. My grandmother had never before left the country and did not possess a passport. (When visiting us in New York, she obsessed about catching germs in public bathrooms.) At seventy years old, she sought out a pilgrimage tour and set off on her great adventure.

This desire, to meet the Mother of God across borders, has be-come a recurring theme in my own life. My grandmother's daring de-parture comprised my first experience of the Virgin Mary's persuasive power to convince devotees to "cross over." Traditionally the Mother of God has possessed an astounding capacity to propel believers to-ward new horizons of encounter.

Since the branches of my family stem from Irish, Italian, and Slovenian Catholic roots, I suppose it is not surprising that I inherited a strong connection to Mary. My grandmother was blessed with an awareness of the holy in everyday life, an awareness that any New Age adherent would envy. The hours of her day were regulated by saying the *Memorare* upon waking, the *Angelus* at noon, and the rosary be-fore bed. My grandmother, it seemed, spoke with the Virgin Mary on a daily basis.

I have held my own ongoing conversation with the Mother of God for most of my life, but mine has more resembled an argument.

My grandmother's devotion was of a European-American immi-grant style whose time had passed. Vatican II had just reassessed the place of the Virgin Mary in ecclesial life—with the unintended effect of not only curtailing excesses but also dampening appropriate ex-pressions of genuine devotion. On a cultural level, assigned as it was to the private sphere, Marian veneration among European-American Catholics waned as the domestic realm itself diminished in impor-tance. Vibrancy of devotion to the Mother of God faded while mothers entered the workforce in unprecedented numbers. Traditional images of the Mother of God seemed to promote a return to a family life that appeared more and more archaic. Did the Virgin Mary have contemporary relevance at all?

My mother's generation was faced with an even more unsettling question. The light of the women's movement had exposed underlying patterns that led me to question the role of Mary in a way that had simply never occurred to my grandmother. Gender roles were changing significantly, and the complementarity of the sexes—so taken for granted under the rubric of devotion to Mary—was rightfully being challenged by ideas of expanded social relationships.

Feminism exposed with painful insightfulness how the Mother of God has been used *against* women. As both virgin and mother, Mary has been held up as an impossible model whose unattainable singularity must nevertheless be emulated. The title of Marina Warner's illuminating but ultimately devastating book on Marian development throughout the centuries succinctly captures the historical reality: Mary went from being "blessed among women" to "alone of all her sex." Feminist scholars seemed to be asking, *Should* traditional interpretations of Mary be held up as relevant?

My mother's spirituality was different from my grandmother's and tended toward the monastic. Although my mother initially considered joining a religious order, her life's calling led her to the Catholic Worker. She left her parents to join Dorothy Day in New York, where she met my father over a huge pot in a soup kitchen. My father, a working-class Catholic of Italian and Irish background, had devoted his life to the peace movement and organized the first protest against the Vietnam War. My mother, brother, and I lived at a Catholic Worker Farm while my father served time in prison for burning his draft card (I took my first steps in a prison waiting room on visiting day).

My brother and I grew up in a small interracial city while my father took faith-based delegations for peace over the globe—a modern version of pilgrimage. The traditional devotions of my grandparents' generation seemed quaintly irrelevant as I grew in understanding of my father's political activism. My mother sustained her contemplative nature through religious music and art. For a brief time, she convinced us to pray Compline each night, ending with *Salve Regina* in Latin. But, by and large, the brokenness I had already perceived in the world appeared too fierce a match for the mild Virgin Mary, who obviously knew nothing of nuclear threat, race riots in our high school, or "disappeared" church workers in Central America.

Deprived of the cultural milieu which had made them so satisfying for immigrant Catholics of my grandmother's generation, the sentimental pictures and plaster statues of the Virgin Mary—far removed from the messy realities of women and men of flesh and blood—rendered her lifeless. The post–Vatican II Catholic Church in the United States, it seemed, had not yet decided what to do about Mary, and so my generation grew up impoverished compared to the rich and multifaceted Marian traditions of other time periods or of other parts of the Catholic world.

The chasm between the stereotypically passive Marian image about which I learned from the Polish religious sisters in our parochial school and my nascent desire (in that lovely Jewish expression) "to repair the world" was bridged in a notable occurrence during my adolescent years. My father had taken a job directing a soup kitchen, and we moved into a vacant three-story brick convent building. In Catholic Worker style, my parents began to take in homeless guests. My mother named our house of hospitality in honor of her mother's favorite Madonna. A picture of Our Lady of Guadalupe stood at the door to receive those who crossed its threshold.

I chose a women's college, where I stopped going to Mass. I studied anthropology, hungering for a gender-affirming spirituality that I sensed was absent from my religious tradition. One day, my favorite professor—a practicing Jew who is an expert in Hinduism—lectured on the Virgin Mary as a form of "female symbolic power." During her presentation, the professor introduced the lyrics to the medieval sailors' hymn, *"Ave Maris Stella."* In her view, the presence of a female figure allows Christian women and men an expanded symbolic repertoire for experiencing and articulating religious expressions that draw upon gender-based metaphors.

Once I understood that the problem is not only what Mary does to *us* but what *we* do to *her,* I was hooked. I set out to take her seriously, realizing for the first time that authentic interpretations of the symbols that we love are worth fighting for.

The lacuna in my upbringing now made me gratefully receptive to representations of Mary from other cultures. The tenor of my conversation with Mary (really, still more of a monologue) began to change even more as I underwent my first experiences in Latin America, where the overpowering maternal figure of the Virgin Mary acquires strength and vitality from popular traditions—some rooted in centuries-old devotions with indigenous precedents, others stemming from more recent currents such as liberation theology.

The Mother of God became "real" for me during these encounters. In Mexico City, I traced my grandmother's steps: I went to the basilica and met Our Lady of Guadalupe. When I saw the multitudes of pilgrims praying there on their knees, something moved deep within me. A sense of profound, wordless connection with other seekers overwhelmed me, as did the image itself. With its timeless, tender intimacy, the Virgin's face seemed to communicate an immediate mission with passionate intensity.

This encounter connected me with my family's faith inheritance, placing me in a chain of generations of believers; at the same time, it was a highly charged personal experience. I would go so far as to say that this first visit to the basilica served as the single most empowering religious experience I had as a young woman. My devotion to the Virgin of Guadalupe—which was to grow stronger in subsequent years—brought me back to the Christian faith that I had considered leaving behind.

Motivated by my rediscovery of the Mother of God, I went on to do graduate work in Mariology. While not losing my dissatisfaction with my own culture's patterns of male-centered interpretations of Marian tradition—which abound in Latin America, under a different paradigm—I was drawn more and more deeply to seek the face of the Mother of God as a pilgrim in *tierra ajena*, land foreign to me. In Nicaragua, I discovered base ecclesial communities where the traditional image of the Virgin Mary was being reformulated to reflect her role as a fellow disciple in the Reign of God. Along quite different lines, in Mexico, I became enamored of popular religion as practiced in village life—in which the Virgin Mary figures prominently.

Christians have always regarded Mary as too important to leave to theologians; much of the Marian treasury originated in the *sensus fidelium*, the faith of the people. Patroness of the hierarchical Catholic Church, Mary also plays this role for the masses of believers who seek her intercession. Sinners, the sick, those with special petitions and desperate causes, the very young and the very old—all find a place in her favor.

As Mary's is "the face that most resembles Christ's," it is fitting that many parallel Marian devotions and doctrines developed to mirror his (the Immaculate Conception and the Virgin Birth, the Assumption and the Ascension). As a female image, the figure of the Virgin Mary can access a whole world of symbolism in order to describe these beliefs in vivid imagery that would otherwise be lost to us. Many mainline Protestant theologians are turning toward Mary for a feminine face missing in their own traditions.

It no longer sounds radical to assert, as Edward Schillebeeckx did in 1954, that Mary reveals the maternal love of God the Father. Neither is it considered academically outlandish to state that metaphors that are cast in female imagery and that properly refer to the Godhead have migrated to the figure of the historical person of Mary of Nazareth. Systematic theologians like Elizabeth Johnson are now sorting out the dilemma of a human woman being asked to represent through the centuries, as it is now commonly phrased, "the feminine face of God."

Putting this doctrinal dilemma aside, there is no question regarding the fact that Marian studies have been enriched in recent decades by historical and scriptural exploration.

As a member of the Communion of Saints, Mary of Nazareth belongs to the universal church; astoundingly, her influence extends even beyond the bounds of Christianity (Muslims, for example, respect her courage and fidelity, as reported in their own holy writings). The Assumption removed Mary, body and soul, from this planet, paradoxically making her accessible to the whole world: unlike veneration of local saints or martyrs in the early church, veneration of Christ's mother could not be confined to a single commemoration site. From the beginning of the history of Marian devotion, the Virgin has crossed barriers to attend to the generations of believers entrusted to her, according to St. John's gospel, at the foot of the cross. In tradition, she ushers devotees over that final border that all humans traverse at the end of their earthly pilgrimages.

As early as the time in which the gospels were written, the figure of the mother of Jesus—portrayed in St. Luke's gospel through her key role in the infancy narratives and her depiction as model disciple—became associated with the believing community that announces the Word. As mother of the church, Mary's nurturing role leads her to disregard geographical and cultural barriers in order to enter more deeply into human lives shaped by these very boundaries. As a universal figure, Mary transcends borders, but as a local patroness she envelops the *people* they define in an embrace so close that her very identity melds into theirs.

Down through the centuries, the Virgin Mary has accompanied local churches in their particular pilgrimages toward salvation, most notably by taking on the character and even the countenance of their people. This personification is especially evident in the image of the Virgin of Guadalupe, whose figure represents a crossover between European and indigenous symbolism and who embodies a distinctly Latin American face of Christianity.

The ongoing popularity of Marian pilgrimage centers reflects the conviction held by generations of Christians that the Virgin's maternal advocacy can be sought and gained through their own journeys. In our seemingly secularized world, higher numbers of devotees are flocking to Marian shrines than at any other time in history.

Herself a pilgrim, the Virgin Mary arrives, as San Salvador's Archbishop Oscar Romero poetically summarized in a homily given on the Virgin of Guadalupe's feast day, "*al alma del pueblo,*" "at the people's soul." Nowhere is this more apparent than in the realm of popular religion. Defined by theologian Virgilio Elizondo as the body of traditions practiced by believers at large, expressing the deepest identity of a people in its attitudes and practices, popular piety gives witness to the belief that the Mother of God can be encountered as a living presence.

Apparition stories rooted in the past, such as the one in which the Virgin of Guadalupe appeared to St. Juan Diego Cuauhtlatoatzin, often serve as foundational narratives for contemporary personal and collective devotion.

In Catholic tradition, apparitions tend to follow certain patterns, and the apparitions in Latin America during the Conquest and colonial periods follow an even tighter symbolic structure. Spanish Marian apparition stories often feature either shepherds or children, thus portraying Mary as seeking out society's most vulnerable and least valued. For example, the Spanish Guadalupan apparition story tells of a cowherd finding a buried Black Madonna statue which, according to legend, had been hidden from the iconoclastic Moors.

Latin American apparition stories incorporate an ethnic element in which the identity of the visionary plays a pivotal role. Peru's *Señor de los Milagros*, the Lord of Miracles, was painted by an African-Peruvian visionary; the devotion to this dark-skinned Christ on the Cross thrived among indigenous, black, *mulatto*, and *mestizo* Catholics before eventually being sanctioned by the ethnically Spanish hierarchy. Some portrayals of *La Virgen de la Caridad del Cobre*, an image of Mary in Cuba, show her appearing to three fishermen: one black, one Indian, and one Spanish. Numerous apparitions of virgins in colonial Mexico (Ocotlán in Tlaxcala, Remedios in Mexico, San Juan de los Lagos and Zapópan in Jalisco) cast indigenous converts as protagonists. These events—whatever their historical validity—signify the "appearance" of Christianity in the Americas.

In modern times, thousands of Marian apparitions are reported to the Vatican each year from diverse parts of the world, but those that gain popular local acceptance and (perhaps) eventually some level of ecclesial acknowledgment tend to arise in areas dominated by social upheaval or conflict. The apparitions at Medjugorie, for example, in the former Yugoslavia, take place in a rural village in a historically war-torn area where construction of the town's church building was paid for by remittances sent home by emigrants working abroad in Italy or Germany. In cases such as this one, the personal encounter of a visionary or group of visionaries garners momentum from a collective situation of vulnerability that makes the wider community receptive, as well, to the occurrence of an apparition. Whether outsiders find these experiences credible or not (belief in apparitions is not required by Catholic doctrine, belonging, rather, to the realm of private revelation), apparitions *do* reveal belief in the Virgin Mary's presence.

Apparitions, of course, are all about seeing: glimpsing a spiritual reality that always exists yet is not readily or consistently visible. Privileged moments in which the intangible object of devotion is grasped visually, apparitions momentarily rend the veil between the material and supernatural worlds. As a member of the Communion of Saints, the Virgin Mary enjoys eternal life and is mysteriously present among us; however, we do not *see* her. Nor do we usually experience ourselves as *being seen* by her—though every Catholic child is taught that her maternal presence hovers over us, perpetually, in solicitous watch. A temporary respite from our blindness to spiritual reality, the apparition enacts a mutual event in which the visionary and the receiving community experience both *seeing* and *being seen*. The dynamic is one of divine initiative and human receptivity. This sense of vital relationship, of *being seen* by heavenly eyes even in the most desperate of circumstances, contradicts modern sensibility. In dominant Western culture, we are raised with a *scientific* worldview, thus losing the religious imagination which, historically, Christians with a *symbolic* worldview took (and take) for granted.

For Catholic children, familiar with statues and pictures of Mary from early childhood, the figure of the Mother of God becomes more than simply a visual stimulus; representations of the Virgin Mary convey the presence of a living being with whom they enter into relationship. For example, the emotive bonding between the Virgin of Guadalupe and believers largely takes place through the use of religious images. Representations of the Mother of God cast in familiar iconography made meaningful by their cultural setting "speak" to believers, for example, to my grandmother in Ohio and to me in Mexico City.

In making the presence of the Virgin Mary (or of the saints, or of Christ) palpable, statues and pictures that in effect blur the barrier between the material and the spiritual are assigned a privileged place by popular religion. The Virgin of Guadalupe provides a breathtaking example of the power of religious images to communicate the Mother of God's maternal care expressed in language and symbolism that is deeply meaningful to adherents. The original painting, which my grandmother and I both visited in Mexico City, is regarded as miraculous in itself.

Upon completing my studies, shortly after the birth of our eldest daughter, my husband and I returned to New York. We got to know members of immigrant communities in the Hudson River Valley through our work in a Spanish-speaking parish and in a migrant health clinic.

Over the years, we heard stories of suffering and courage from people whose testimonies awakened my own faith. In their most difficult moments, when overcome by feelings of depression or loneliness or the seemingly insurmountable obstacles that faced them, they knew they were not alone: God—often through the advocacy of the

Virgin Mary—was with them. Some expressed this realization as a momentary, piercing insight to which they would cling for months or years once the intensity of experience had faded; others spoke of it as a certainty that they could grasp, a constant, sustaining thread that gave cohesion to their lives.

Immersed in a community that I loved and that loved *her*, I began to speak less and to listen more. Guided by mentors whose patience never ceases to amaze me, I learned to tread on holy ground where I had to take the proverbial sandals off my feet. My appreciation of the Virgin Mary—based on new insights and interpretations— grew. As the biblical Mary of Nazareth accepted God's invitation to become a mother, in tradition, the Mother of God becomes available to those who would know her. One of the venues of availability is through images.

In our ministry, I soon became aware of cultural differences in our perceptions of religious art. The presence and importance of images, for me, was secondary, but for the people we accompanied, images were indispensable. At one prayer session at a farm-worker camp, my husband and I arrived to find that the large reproduction of the image of the Virgin that we routinely used had been moved prematurely to another camp. The migrants present (some sixty men from four different farms) would not pray until a wallet-sized holy card with the Virgin's image had been brought forward.

I have found that the popular Latin American attitude toward religious images is more akin to the Eastern Orthodox spirituality of icons than to the Western view of religious art. An icon is not intended to be a work of art or even a life-like portrait, but rather a window to the sacred, a holy item that will be used in devotions or in liturgy; the representations in this type of art follow prescribed patterns rather than expressing individual artistic innovation.

A popular story summarizes nicely the proper devotional attitude toward icons. A Russian peasant had in her possession a fine icon of great value. Art historians, having heard rumors of its existence, with effort located the woman in her remote village and asked her to sell the icon to a museum collection. When the woman refused their monetary offers, they realized that she was not interested in financial gain, so they changed their line of argument, urging that if she really cared about the icon, she would want its beauty to be seen and enjoyed by all. Her answer, "But who will *pray* with it?" leads to the conclusion that it is better for one person to contemplate an icon than for thousands merely to see it.

Since the Virgin Mary was the instrument through whom God realized the Incarnation, it is fitting that the Mother of God figure prominently in iconography. The names of Marian representations suggest their different characters: All-Holy Virgin; Sweetly-Kissing Mother; Celestial Ladder between Heaven and Earth; She Who Is Wider than the Heavens.

One of the most ancient and beloved representations, *Theotokos*, "God-Bearer," carries its own history as to how the title originated. When a fifth-century theologian proposed changing the term to *Christotokos*, "Christ-Bearer," the Council of Ephesus vehemently defended the original title, whose literal translation might be rendered "The One who Gave Birth to the One who is God."[1] The Virgin of Guadalupe—a mother who speaks to St. Juan Diego Cuauhtlatoatzin in his own native language and who communicates her maternity through indigenous terms and symbols—invites all believers (colonial and modern) to a deeper relationship with her, and through her, with the God in her womb.

In the foundational narrative, the Virgin of Guadalupe reveals herself as mother of Juan Diego Cuauhtlatoatzin; of all those who inhabit the Americas (at that time, native nations); and of all who share in the devotion to Mary. In ever-expanding circles, her patronage begins with one specific encounter and then spreads in an embrace that extends across borders and through time. She acts as a mother for Mexican and Mexican-American Catholics—and for other Latin American and Latino Catholics, and even for non-Latinos. As Empress of the Americas, she plays a special role on both sides of the border. The trademark iconography of *la Guadalupana* has become as visible in Mexican immigrant communities in the North as it is in Mexico.

Lest devotees remain simply mesmerized by her tenderness, this representation of the Virgin Mary—when taken in its context—calls for recognition of her strength, as well. The Guadalupan story confronts a complacent church in the North with what might be considered a pan-American rendition of the Magnificat. The aspect of challenge inherent to this devotion is made clear by a contemporary innovative adaptation of the traditional *Antorcha*, the running relay of a lit torch from the basilica in Mexico City to faith communities on both sides of the border.

The young Jewish woman who broke social convention when she boldly "traveled in haste to the hill country" (Luke 1:39) bearing news of the Incarnation continues to journey. Just as other waves of Catholic immigrants introduced meaningful representations from their countries of origin to local churches, the importation of these devotions signal a tradition that gains strength—rather than losing it—through migration. Placing her steps alongside those of migrants making their way across borders, the Virgin Mary today reveals images of her face which were previously unknown in the North.

The fact that the three images in this book come from traditional Mexican piety will be, I hope, of interest to both Latino and non-Latino readers. As the world's second largest Catholic country, Mexico shares many patterns of traditional religion with other Latin American countries. In the United States, the Mexican and Mexican-American population has multiplied many times over in recent years; a virgin who crosses borders belongs to people who cross borders. In the United States, Latinos currently comprise roughly half of the Catholic Church—and an even larger proportion of the population of young Catholics who will determine its future.

While I do not mean to suggest that all Mexicans and Mexican-Americans do or should practice Catholic popular religion—many other expressions of spirituality certainly exist on both sides of the border—nevertheless, I am convinced that these Marian representations have much to offer the wider church. Maddeningly, the influx of Latin Americans into areas that have not previously experienced Spanish- or Portuguese-speaking waves of immigration in significant numbers is routinely perceived as a pastoral "problem"—instead of as a rich resource with the capacity to revitalize and even correct local churches, bringing them to fuller communion with the universal church.

Emigration can rightfully be called a curse, in that it stems from poverty and oppression and divides families and communities, but migrants and immigrants themselves—with the spiritual dynamism they generate—can become a medium of grace. As one Mexican biblical scholar notes, "migrants are bearers of faith and culture; they are not a problem to be solved, but rather, a blessing to be assumed."[2]

Ironically, just as the Guadalupan message reaches the churches in the North, the churches in the South are undergoing foundational changes. While I had been carrying on my debate with Mary, the argument that is currently causing consternation in Latino and Latin American communities derives from a different sphere. The Protestant Reformation is reaching Latin America as if for the first time. One proselytizer in Brazil boasted optimistically that fully a quarter of the world's largest Catholic country would soon be non-Catholic. While mainline Protestant denominations *are* growing (an entirely new development in historically Roman Catholic–dominated Latin America), the phenomenon is markedly more dramatic in numbers among evangelical Pentecostals. Not unified by any one denomination and therefore not bound to any single overarching structure, these churches vary widely in practices but nevertheless share certain characteristics. Foremost among them—and a cornerstone of Pentecostal spirituality—is the emphatic rejection of religious images, including and especially those of the Virgin Mary.

Of course, popular religion can have its own pitfalls. In official doctrine, religious artifacts refer to divine reality but do not *in themselves* constitute divinity—a belief blurred in the popular religious practice. In addition to ascribing a literal rather than symbolic meaning to religious art, it tends to confuse the intercessory role of the saints with the absolute agency of God. Mainline Catholic theology maintains a sharp distinction between veneration of the saints—including the Virgin Mary—and the adoration of the persons of the Trinity. The former receive *doulia*, honor, with the Queen of the Communion of Saints meriting *hyperdoulia*; but God alone (Father, Son, and Holy Spirit) deserves worship.

This ground has been worked and reworked by theologians, so instead of presenting apologetic or catechetical arguments, I return to the subject of icons. As noted earlier, representations of the saints serve as windows to the sacred—much as the lives of these holy men and women reflected divine grace while they lived, allowing a temporal glimpse into the eternal heart of God. Religious images of the Virgin Mary invite the believing community to a collective mysticism, a communal contemplative encounter with the Mother of God—and, through her, with the Godhead.

The controversy over religious images helped me arrive at a solution to my ambivalence. In my own way, I wondered, hadn't I viewed Mary as a lifeless image—instead of as a living member of the Communion of Saints? Had I not been fundamentalist in looking for biblical texts or images that measured up to my criteria, instead of allowing them to "speak" to me symbolically? The fact was that I had indeed been judging interpretations as acceptable or unacceptable. There is, of course, nothing wrong with this. The exercise of judgment is a necessary enterprise. However, it is not an end in itself. Like others who love Mary, I found that it was only by my actually engaging with the scriptural texts and participating in the liturgical life of a local church that she came alive for me. My relationship with Mary had come full circle: from a personal connection with her as a child under my pious grandmother's influence, to skepticism as a young woman, to rediscovery of Mary's potential meanings in new settings, to a personal relationship—exercised in collectivity—which (I hope) will mature as I mature.

Mary's capacity for contemplation, celebrated in St. Luke's gospel, sets the tone for my own meditation: I continue to "ponder these things in [my] heart" (2:51b). Meeting new images of the Virgin Mary and reflecting on the Mother of God in a different geographical location have enriched my ongoing relationship with the woman who urges believers toward expanded horizons.

* * * * *

After several years of working with immigrant communities in New York State, my husband and I came to realize that if we were to continue to accompany migrant and immigrant communities in New York, we needed to deepen our understanding of Latin American realities—and integrate our children in this mission, as well. We completed a preparatory training with Maryknoll Lay Missioners and in 2004, moved with our (then) three children to the southern state of Oaxaca in Mexico.

In Oaxaca, I discovered a rich Marian tradition in the Virgin of Juquila. This unofficial patroness of migrants draws pilgrims in droves on the arduous journey to her sanctuary. The fervor that this representation awakens in devotees taught me much about Oaxaca itself.

In contrast, my homesickness while living abroad led me to reflect on the huge role of the Virgin of Guadalupe in New York's Mexican communities. Visits to several sending communities in Puebla and Oaxaca further inspired my reflection.

Moving to Oaxaca had meant leaving behind immigrant communities that were dear to me; in the midst of my loss I found the Virgin of Solitude. During our third year in Oaxaca, civil unrest broke out, causing many deaths and resulting in a state of emergency that lasted for months. My encounter with the image of the Mother of God at the foot of the cross seemed an appropriate meeting, given its timing.

In the three representations of the Mother of God that I explore in this book, the particularly Latin American emphasis on the Virgin *as mother* comes to the fore. And . . . my own role as mother changed drastically. After a high-risk pregnancy (my doctor was "99 percent sure" that it would not come to term), I gave birth to our fourth and fifth children: twin girls.

Parenting in our home country is challenging enough, but having twins in Mexico—while simultaneously raising their three older siblings—both challenged and blessed our family more than I could have imagined. The outpouring of support and encouragement we received was as overwhelming as the task of caring for not one but *two* newborns. As parents of twins can attest, the simplest acts of daily life become exponentially more complicated. On the other hand, missioner families famously gain entry into receiving cultures through their children; our older children's acculturation process accelerated

Deirdre Cornell, Kenney Gould, and children at Santo Domingo Church, Oaxaca

our own, and the twins' arrival cemented more thoroughly our local relationships.

Our mission placement provided a setting in which parenting is given social priority and in which the Mother of God is a visible affirmation of the maternal role.

Daily life in southern Mexico, although changing rapidly with globalization, is still patterned on the rhythm of religious practice. Finding myself surrounded by images of Mary in multiple forms in Oaxaca's traditionally Catholic society, I encountered her face everywhere. Our family was living in a marginal neighborhood on the outskirts of the capital, where I volunteered in our parish and my husband in a health clinic. We were immersed in an environment that was poor in material resources but rich in faith.

My grandmother's generation "met" Mary through both communal and home-centered veneration. Rosary crusades that filled sports stadiums allowed Catholic European-American (mostly working-class) immigrants to feel strength in numbers—and to make their presence known to a society that still did not completely accept them. Decades later, like other post–Vatican II Catholics, I did not inherit their version of *communitas;* for me, the insertion of my private, devotional family life into a public setting steeped in Christian customs was a novel experience.

In Oaxaca, Mary came alive for me in a whole new way, taking on flesh in a shared collective mysticism. I nursed our infants under a *rebozo,* a traditional shawl, as I researched customs about the Virgin's veil. Our daughters took their first steps while pilgrims to Juquila walked past our front door and uttered their first word ("Mamá") as I pondered Mary's silence. And while the escalating social conflict in Oaxaca gripped my whole being with a desperate urge to protect my children, it also led me to meditate on the image of a Mother standing at the foot of her Son's cross.

I have often marveled that my grandmother found in the Virgin Mary a replacement for her own mother, whom she lost at the age of twelve (when she herself stood poised at the threshold of womanhood) to a degenerative terminal illness. On a sentimental level, for individual Christians the image of a heavenly mother evokes the surfacing of emotions related to psychological needs, such as reassurance and security. (Conversely, those with negative or ambivalent personal associations of their own mothers might have an adverse reaction.)

The three images of Mary at an adobe home in Huayapam, Oaxaca

When regarded in fuller historical and iconographic contexts, however, images of the Mother of God plumb even greater depths. In collective settings, Latin American popular religious practice lends vitality to communally revered religious images. Social construction lends to Mary's motherhood a cultural power that surpasses individual experiences—a total that is more than the sum of its parts. The maternity of the Virgin Mary taps into the emotional lives of devotees, but her real strength is drawn from a realm found beyond simply interpersonal relationships (as important as these are). Marian imagery mines a mother lode.

Comparisons of maternal types are best left to Latino (and, even better, to Latin*a*) psychologists, who can probe with more accurate insight both the positive and detrimental aspects of cultural patterns on both sides of the border.[3] However, what can be admitted as a generalization is that the role of mothers in Latino and Latin American communities—undeniably complicated as it is—carries more weight than does that of their U.S. dominant-culture counterparts.

In Latin America, the familial parenting role—especially that of mothers—spills over into public life more visibly than in the United States. The title *padres de familia* (which includes both genders) has no real English equivalent, but in Mexico denotes a publicly acknowledged civic role.[4] In her research with Mexican-American women on the Virgin of Guadalupe, theologian Jeanette Rodriguez found that Mother's Day ranked as one of the highest rated holidays of the year. A truism often expressed is that mothers are such a wonderful invention, even God wanted to have one!

Any emphasis on Mary's maternity comes with inherent risk. Elizabeth Johnson outlines how Marian devotion has been used to maintain women in subordinate and truncated roles, predominantly maternal ones; Jeanette Rodriguez sharply notes that Mexican-American

Seamus, Rosa, Rachel, Rebecca, and Thomas Gould at the Soledad Basilica

women deserve more than "a long-suffering mother, wrapped in blue and set up on a pedestal."[5]

My ongoing internal conversation with the Mother of God has reflected this struggle. What could she, a perfect wife and mother, know of my ambivalence in dealing with career and family? How can her image—so often cast as docile and passive—empower believers? When such questions are asked from the perspective of people living south of the border, they take on an even more critical edge: What does the Queen of Heaven offer a widow raising eleven children in a shantytown?

Female imagery *in itself* has not been shown historically to guarantee social—or even gender—equality (e.g., the ancient cult of Isis, identified with theocracy, justified slavery, war, and human sacrifice). And Marian interpretations that arise in male-dominated societies tend to copy repressive and socially determined gender roles in the religious sphere.

With this caveat having been stated, it is clear that Mary's maternal role in salvation history has served as a sign of hope and inspiration for Christians over the centuries.

Popular traditions find in the Virgin Mary a protective figure who, like Christ, "desired to gather [Jerusalem's] children together as a hen gathers her brood under her wings" (Matthew 23:37). Devotion to the Virgin of Juquila, represented by a diminutive statue of the Virgin Mary in Oaxaca whose popularity is currently multiplying exponentially, vividly reflects the meaning of this scriptural verse. Pilgrims reach the culmination of their journey when they pass, literally, under the Virgin's mantle.

As a patroness of travelers, this little-studied but well-established image lends herself to pilgrimage and to internal and foreign migration. Here we find an example of how a local devotion can spread with remarkable success regionally and even internationally when its symbolism "fits" the life situations of adherents. Often perceived as static and unchanging, in fact, popular devotions as cultural customs—unfettered as they are by institutional control—can adapt relatively quickly according to the motivations of those who practice them. (Between the time I began and finished this manuscript, in two local parishes here in New York, Mexican devotees have begun to offer Mass in honor of the Virgin of Juquila on her feast day.)

In the three devotions that I describe in this book, the role of the Virgin Mary as mother intersects with her identity as symbol of *communitas*. Anthropologists Victor and Edith Turner describe *communitas* as the collective underpinnings that hold a society together. Particular representations of the Mother of God attract devotees when they resonate deeply with a culture's (or cultures') spirituality—paradoxically, thus gaining power to cross the boundaries of the very cultures from which they arise. This dynamism is expressed tangibly through pilgrimage, in which travelers brave obstacles—borders—in seeking the object of their devotion. Even the most dangerous pilgrimage ends in a homecoming when pilgrims reach their goal. Drawn close by a heavenly mother, believers find in the Virgin's tangible imagery experiences leading to encounter with the divine.

When it is not possible for devotees to visit a sanctuary (as in the case of undocumented Latin Americans in the United States who do not dare to leave the country), they must invent creative ways to approximate the spiritual experiences that pilgrimage inspires—and to establish the devotion in their new homeland. In New York, *guadalupanos* have opened new paths of fervor in bearing the *Antorcha* to parishes that were previously unfamiliar with this custom. Local churches have been enriched by recent Mexican immigration and the devotional practices that crossed the border with the immigrants (summed up by the pithy title of one anthropological study, *Guadalupe in New York*[6]).

Reproductions of religious images of the Virgin Mary serve as strong triggers of devotion, for they "awaken" a relationship that all too often lies dormant. Images can transport Christian believers to a spiritual state in which they are nurtured and empowered to grow as people of faith. As Christianity's most beloved (and most often depicted) saint, the Mother of God offers many faces upon which we can gaze; in this mutual *seeing*, our deepest identities are affirmed. We know ourselves for who we truly are, mirrored in a mother's eyes.

Perhaps my own most illuminating insight into the Madonna's motherhood came in simply contemplating our infant daughters' faces. On the wall behind the rocking chair where I nursed, I taped a small reproduction of Rafael Boticelli's *Madonna and Child*. This lovely, plump mother with her peaceful smile and the rosy child held loosely but tenderly seemed exactly the right image for our first exhausting, exhilarating weeks. While my own face was the first with which my daughters became acquainted, the Virgin Mary's was soon to follow.

The first significant event in a baby's life is gazing into his or her mother's eyes. The most potent visual stimulus in an infant's environment, a mother's expressive face literally awakens a newborn's consciousness.

Across cultures, a mother instinctively tends to place an infant at the left breast—closer to the soothing sound of her heartbeat and situated at the perfect angle for visual interaction. A newborn's range of vision measures precisely the distance between his or her eyes and those of the nursing mother.

The attachment or bonding process in which a child becomes emotionally connected to a caregiver begins with periods of intense mutual gaze. These experiences are brief but frequently repeated over the first few months of the infant's life. As time passes, other types of interaction are gradually added (e.g., "baby talk"). While the attachment process is *instinctive*, it is not *automatic*: it depends on active interaction initiated by the caregiver. Other persons in the family setting contribute to this pattern (I have been known to fanatically insist that my older children not "break the gaze" of their newborn siblings), but it is imperative that over the first years of a child's life he or she receive consistent one-on-one attention from a primary caregiver in order for attachment to take place. These interactions have lasting and determining effects on a child's cognitive and psychological development. In the context of intimate relationship, the groundwork for our futures is laid by our mothers' gaze. In a sense, our later lives are records of this original blueprint.[7]

Motherhood is the *real* "oldest profession"; the daily, countless acts that every mother performs for her child comprise the first human experiences of solidarity. The nine months of sheltering, cradling, and nourishing a baby in one's belly under a protective mantle of flesh extend into other nurturing tasks whose lasting value will be played out over the child's lifetime.

Prayer, too, can be an act of solidarity: I know with utmost certainty that every night of my life until she died, my grandmother prayed for me. Sometimes I feel as if her rogation cloaks me posthumously—whether because prayer transcends the limits of time and space or due to her elevated position in the Communion of Saints, I don't know. What I *do* know is that her prayer still covers me, a blessing over the years of my life to come.

* * * * *

The Jesuit church that looms a block off Oaxaca City's main plaza houses a purportedly miraculous image of Christ on the way to Calvary. The official title of the church honors the Immaculate Conception of the Virgin Mary.[8] My attraction to this church came neither from the bloody, long-haired statue encased behind glass where, like so many others, I crammed photos of my children, nor from the church's noble role in the tense (also bloody) conflict that dominated our last year in Oaxaca. The seat of gravity, for me, was a side altar honoring *Nuestra Señora de Guadalupe*, "Our Lady of Guadalupe," also called *la Virgen de Guadalupe*. The walls, painted with words that must be approached in order to be deciphered, beckon like whispers. Stenciled on plaster and framed by decorative borders, these words relay an identical message in Nahuatl, Huaves, Chatino, Cuicateco, Spanish, Mazateco, Amuzgo, Chinanteco, Triqui, English, one variation of Mixtec, and four of Zapotec. Different languages pose a single rhetorical question: "*Cu ix amó nican nicá nimo nantzin*," "Am I not here, who am your mother?"

The representation of Our Lady of Guadalupe in this side altar may not be particularly noteworthy for its artistic value; nevertheless, it achieves its purpose. Faithful to the iconography of the original image, the Virgin's figure is immediately identifiable by her warm skin color and the clues of the Immaculate Conception motif. Mary stands poised astride the silver curves of the crescent moon as if riding into heaven; golden rays frame the contours of her body as if her form were superimposed on the sun. The red robe, etched with a vine and leaf pattern, is topped by a graceful blue mantle, and the stars and gold trim of the outfit enhance her celestial appearance. A black belt is tied around her waist, and, easily overlooked in the scrimshaw pattern of her robe, a single, four-petalled flower sits over her womb. Mary's reassuring facial expression and hands folded delicately in prayer finish the image's overall effect.

Contemplating the words and image together never failed to move me. Like studying a family photo while on a long journey, looking at the Virgin of Guadalupe in this side altar both grieved and sustained me far from home. It grieved me because the familiarity of her icon sharpened my homesickness; it sustained me because, somehow—in the interaction between my longing and the divine presence mediated through the image—I emerged whole again, strengthened for whatever lay ahead.

And what lay ahead was challenging. In Oaxaca, the communities with which our lay missioner organization worked were soon to come into grave danger. In 2006, the capital and other parts of the state were convulsed by tumult; the eyes of the world turned toward Oaxaca. On May 22, a week after Teachers' Day, the seventy-thousand-member state chapter of the national teachers' union took over the main plaza of the capital.[9] This type of event had become almost standard procedure, since the union had held sit-ins on the plaza each May for twenty-six years. However, the new governor refused to negotiate labor conditions, and a seven-month stand-off began.

Shifts of teachers and their supporters were taking turns at the plaza on June 14 when, before dawn, state, municipal, and ministerial police forces attacked the encampment. Public outrage surged in support for the union, and by noon, some thirty thousand Oaxacans amassed in the teachers' defense forced police to retreat. In an outpouring of *communitas,* Oaxacans of diverse walks of life from all eight regions joined together in a single, spontaneous demand—namely, that the governor resign.

One community organizer used the image of a pressure cooker to describe what was happening: dissatisfaction with the state government on many different levels inflamed Oaxacan society to its boiling point, causing the lid to blow on June 14. The Popular Assembly of the Peoples of Oaxaca (APPO), a coalition of some 350 trade unions, neighborhood or village committees, small farmers' organizations, civil associations, and indigenous collectives, formed overnight as a counterpart to the teacher's union. Observers compared the phenomenon to Oaxaca's famous *guelaguetza* (indigenous festival of song and dance) for the way it brought together different sectors of society.

At its height, the movement brought a quarter of the state's population to the streets: between eight hundred thousand and one million people participated in at least one of several marches. Among other actions, the teachers' union and the Popular Assembly took over the plaza in a huge populist sit-in. Rural and indigenous organizations poured in from other parts of the state to draw attention to their demands—and to the plight of their leaders who had been disappeared or detained. Base ecclesial communities—including the one to which I belonged—set up an impromptu first aid station, soup kitchen, and food pantry in the Jesuit church.

As those grueling months of Oaxaca's state conflict played out, violence escalated. The few cases that I describe in the last chapter are not the conflict's most dramatic murders, but rather, the ones of which I have first-hand knowledge: I translated the testimonies of three widows (along with those of two women prisoners) for human rights workers investigating the conflict in Oaxaca.[10]

Our parish on the outskirts of the capital held the Stations of the Cross each year during Lent. That year, I attended a session led by the base ecclesial communities. Jesus met his mother at the Fourth Station while participants listened to these words:

> Mary continues accompanying her Son who lives and suffers among us. She is present when we struggle each day to provide our families with bread, water, housing, education, and faith . . . Mary accompanies us when we join together to seek whatever is needed for people to live in human dignity. Mary gives strength to so many mothers who work as domestic servants, street vendors, farm workers or factory workers, earning miserable salaries . . . She gives strength to so many mothers who suffer the unjust murders of their children. She is present with the mothers who demand the return of their children or other family members "disappeared" by unjust governments. Virgin Mary, Mother of Jesus and Our Mother, give us the strength to follow your example. Help us to transform the pain of so many mothers into the fervent desire to work so that in our families and communities, our children can grow in a setting of peace, justice and love.[11]

In a portrayal of the Mother of Christ at the foot of the cross, the Virgin Mary comes alive as a distinctly Oaxacan version of the *Mater Dolorosa* or "Sorrowful Mother." Seemingly a barren image, the Virgin of Solitude, through her tears, nourishes the spiritual lives of her devotees through a crossover of popular customs and official liturgical practice. In a larger context, she represents an instance of the interplay between scriptural and traditional sources in the forming of a motif with tremendous capacity to evoke a creative response on the part of believers.

Marian imagery holds a genius for bringing together seemingly irreconcilable polarities. In the beginning, in fecund silence, the Spirit of God (in Hebrew, *Ruah*) hovered over the waters. Silence flowered into speech as God uttered the first words of creation, *"Let there be light."* For Christians, the Virgin Mary symbolizes human receptivity to this same generative Spirit.

But the *Mater Dolorosa* reveals another quality of openness. The Virgin standing beside her crucified Son gazes upon the cosmic power that attempts to *un*do God's creation. Through witnessing the suffering of Jesus, she beholds the depths of evil.

It was during the conflict and its aftermath that I realized the power of the Virgin Mary's famous silence: she is silent in order that we learn to speak. What we perceive—mistakenly—as her passivity is, in fact, her willingness to wait for us, a church on pilgrimage . . . to record our steps toward peace and justice . . . to witness in watchful, hopeful vigil . . . to bring us to birth, and then to birth us into speech.

This receptivity, this witness, evokes *our* articulation of Mary. It is an articulation that requires a return to the sources of Marian devotion in scripture and tradition in order to sift through the plethora of images that surround a woman—to borrow an axiom from the Middle Ages—"about whom enough can never be said." Stereotypical portrayals of Mary may be passive and uncritical, but, in my view, a search for Mary (in writer Sally Cunneen's words, as "the woman and the symbol") must be both passionate and informed.

Virgilio Elizondo cautions that the dominant culture must not equate Latino popular religious practice in the United States with the spirituality of our European-American grandmothers' generation. Readers will, I hope, soon realize (if they have not already) that there are huge cultural differences to be respected—not overlooked—when non-Latino Christians approach images drawn from Latin America of the Mother whom we hold in common. And although my grandmother's devotion initiated my search for Mary, I do not envision a "return" to pre–Vatican II Marianism (even if this were possible) in our post-modern world. My reflections on Mary are enriched by sources that were not available to my grandmother's generation (e.g., contemporary biblical criticism, liberation theology, anthropological studies of Christianity).

Undoubtedly, my view of the Virgin Mary has been most influenced by my participation in Spanish-speaking faith communities in the United States and Mexico. In these communities, I encounter the Virgin Mary of my inheritance in a new way.

As a nineteen-year-old college student on my first trip abroad, I was asked a seemingly simple question that profoundly reconfigured my frame of geography—and my own identity. It was during the decade of conflict in the eighties in Central America, and international visitors flocked from all over the world to join programs and delegations such as the one I attended. On the very night of my arrival, my host family asked, "Where are you from?"

Unthinkingly, I replied, "America."

Without missing a beat, they responded, "So are we. Everyone who is from the Americas is American."

With this simple exchange, the borders in my mind were called into question. I began to see myself as a U.S. American living among Americans of many other countries on a richly diverse, sprawling, *single* continent. The late Pope John Paul II wrote from this perspective when he addressed the apostolic exhortation *Ecclesia in America* to the whole American church, in North, Central, and South America.

My questions have changed. My ongoing argument has been transformed.

Are Catholics in the United States ready to reconsider Mary? Can we from the dominant culture catch new glimpses of our mother—even when she does not look like us—in images that originated beyond our borders? And will contemporary Christians re-envision Mary's role to allow for more powerful, less sentimental images of the Mother of God?

Openness to the divine presence as mediated through the natural world and receptivity to spiritual awakening—long-standing tenets of Christian popular tradition—are particularly timely contributions to an emerging awareness of the fragility of our planet. The use of female images, furthermore, carries the potential (not often realized in world religions) of reshaping our formulations of symbolic language and gender. Today's globalized world begs for spiritualities that can fluidly adapt to shifting cultural, social, and geographic realities—while remaining rooted in time-tested traditions.

A fragment of a forgotten account of the apparition of the Virgin of Guadalupe was rediscovered in a manuscript found, of all places, in New York City's Public Library. Written in Nahuatl over four centuries ago, the words describe a woman who shines "as luster for all the world."

Perhaps the portrait of a Madonna who crosses boundaries, giving life to the gospel, is precisely the image we need.

II

O María, Madre mía,	Oh Mary, my Mother,
O consuelo del mortal	Comfort of the human soul,
Amparadme y guiadme	Shelter me and guide me
A la patria celestial.	To the heavenly abode.

✳ ✳ ✳ ✳ ✳ ✳ ✳ ✳ ✳ ✳ ✳ ✳

Buenos días, Paloma Blanca	Good morning, White Dove
Hoy te vengo a saludar	Standing before the beauty
Saludando a tu belleza	Of your heavenly throne,
En tu reino celestial.	I have come to greet you.
Eres Madre de Creador	Mother of the Creator,
Que a mi corazón encanta	Receive my thanks and love.
Gracias te doy con amor	You have enchanted my heart,
Buenos días, Paloma Blanca.	Good morning, White Dove.
Niña linda, niña santa	Lovely maiden, holy maiden,
Tu dulce nombre alabar	Your sweet name I praise.
Porque eres tan sacrosanta	Because you are immaculate
Hoy te vengo a saludar.	I come to bless your name.
Reluciente como el alba	Resplendent as the sunrise,
Pura, sencilla y sin mancha	Pure and humble, without stain,
¡Que gusto recibe mi alma!	How you gladden my soul!
Buenos días, Paloma Blanca.	Good morning, White Dove, again.

La Virgen de Juquila
The Virgin of Juquila

ON THE ROAD TO JUQUILA

* * * * * * * * * * * * * *

Pilgrimage lives *in Mexico.*
— Victor and Edith Turner

I first learned of *la Virgen de Juquila*, the Virgin of Juquila, in a place about as different from her hometown in rural Oaxaca as one could imagine, the city of New York. During a retreat, participants spoke about a diminutive, miraculous virgin who had accompanied them across the border and whose legendary protection drew them back to give thanks. Over the years I would hear repeatedly about this devotion from immigrants from Puebla, Oaxaca, Guerrero, and Veracruz. My husband and I had traveled extensively through Mexico, but we had never been to Juquila—a small town whose six paved streets are trodden by two million pilgrims a year. How could we not visit the virgin whose veil covered her children on both sides of the border? A friend went so far as to admonish, "If you haven't been to Juquila, you don't know Mexico."

And when we moved to Oaxaca, it seemed I encountered her everywhere. Her triangular-shaped image appears on altars in family businesses and restaurants, and her name is lettered across the windshields of cars, trucks, and buses. A parish in our new neighborhood observed December 8—her feast—in enthusiastic celebration; local residents once saw her appear in a cave on a nearby hillside.

Mostly, I found it impossible not to be stirred by the countless delegations of pilgrims taking the highway through Oaxaca City en route to her sanctuary. All year long, caravans pass through the capital as they make their way toward Santa Catarina Juquila. The pace intensifies in November and does not let up until after the New Year. Fleets of bicyclists block intersections and hundreds of walkers brave

33

the city's treacherous traffic. Usually traveling with a convoy of vehicles that open the way before them and then trail behind them, pilgrim caravans display banners naming the delegation's home community. Mobile shrines—with a statue or framed picture of the Virgin
—are sometimes set up in the back of pick-up trucks to travel along
on the journey. More commonly, the modest gesture of fastening
flowers and a small image to the front of a vehicle will suffice. Sometimes bike riders hang the Virgin's picture on their backs (giving the
unfortunate impression of moving targets).

Only when my family and I undertook the pilgrimage ourselves
could I fathom what travelers must go through to get to Juquila. The
central valleys of Oaxaca lie like a skirt spread flat, surrounded by the
mountainous regions that rise dramatically at its hem. Of course, pilgrims coming from Puebla to the northwest or Veracruz to the northeast have already faced the daunting mountains of the Sierra Norte,
and pilgrims coming from Guerrero (to the west) take an alternate,
coastal route. But regardless of the direction from which pilgrims
come, they must confront peaks rugged enough to dissuade even the
bravest adventurer. In 1524, Hernán Cortés complained of Oaxaca by
letter to the King of Spain, "This land is so mountainous that it cannot even be crossed on foot."

Today, pilgrims converge in Juquila after having walked, driven, or
ridden on roads hewn into the sides of cliffs, roads barely wide enough
to accommodate two vehicles going in opposite directions. Guardrails
and shoulders along the highway are rare. Roadside shrines or crosses
bearing names and dates, adorned with plastic flowers, mark the places
where travelers came to a premature end of their journey.

Mexico is home to a number of religious pilgrimage centers, some
of which are larger or more well known (e.g., the renowned Basilica
of Saint Mary of Guadalupe, the sanctuary of the Lord of Chalma in
the State of Mexico, the church of the Virgin of San Juan de los Lagos
in Jalisco). All of these sites receive pilgrims who must face physical
exertion and potential danger in order to fulfill a promise to visit the
sanctuary they have chosen as their destination. The Basilica of Saint
Mary of Guadalupe, for example, receives the famous walking pilgrimage from Queretaro in which some forty thousand men and
women travel for two to three weeks on foot. Indeed, all pilgrimage
routes imply *some* level of risk and varying degrees of hazardous travel
conditions. But none compares to the roads to Juquila. Every year, at
least one accidental death takes place.

Juquila is located only six or seven hours by car from the capital, but it *feels* centuries removed. The journey itself takes on this character once the city is left behind. Passing through a series of small towns with all the attributes of village life—corn fields, animals, colonial plazas with churches on one side and municipal offices on the other— the road to Juquila initiates travelers into an excursion through *la provincia*, the country.

Past Zaachila, the lull of a long road trip sets in. I love the stretch of highway lined with oak trees that pleasantly shade the road just before Zimatlán. After the dull grey and brown of the city, the multiple shades of green and colors of flowering vegetation are a welcome sight. Even in the dust of the dry season, I breathe more freely on this road than in the city. Once past Sola de Vega, the steady climb into the cool heights of the Sierra Sur mountains begins.

Sometimes we drive an alternate route. Going north to Tlaxiaco, we head west and traverse part of the Mixteca to make our way down to the coastal highway that eventually connects with a thirty-six-mile dirt road leading into the mountains. On this route, we cross several distinct indigenous territories before arriving at Juquila, located in the heart of Chatino country. Along the way I watch for the changes in women's clothes that signal entry into different ethnically defined areas. In the chilly heights of the Sierra, Triqui women (even little girls) wear thick, intricately woven red mantles over their clothes. By the time we descend the mountains into San Pedro Amuzgo, the climate has turned hot and humid. The Amuzgo women—also renowned weavers—wear dresses of white muslin bordered by brightly colored ribbons. When we arrive at Jamiltepec just north of Puerto Escondido, we see coastal Mixtec women wearing long purple and burgundy striped skirts topped lightly by white shawls.

Whichever route we choose, the roads to Juquila take us through one of Oaxaca's natural treasures, the *mesofilo* forest. The Pacific Ocean comes into view, and we linger in a unique biosphere where humid, salty ocean air mixes with aromatic cold breezes of alpine forests. A tropical climate meets mountains stretching five thousand feet above sea level.

Although nestled in the formidable mountains of the Sierra Sur, one of Oaxaca's eight regions, Juquila technically belongs to the Coast.[1] Its inhabitants share many cultural features such as foods (its *mole* and its coconut desserts, fried plantains, iguana, and armadillo) and music (coastal *chilenas*) with their counterparts closer to the shoreline.

Approaching from the capital, the proximity of the ocean is over-shadowed by the abundance of sweet water in the countryside around Juquila. Along the roadside—even after the year's rains have subsided—water seeps through stone cliffs and trickles down green slopes. Moss grows on rocks; ferns lace the floors of pine forests. The Atoyac River winds all the way down from the capital—gaining momentum once it leaves the polluted city—and turns into the Verde River, which feeds into the Chacahua Bay and empties into the Pacific Ocean. In the woods, small brooks ripple with clear, chilly water, and in Yaitepec two waterfalls cascade.

By now there is less traffic and the only other travelers on the road are fellow pilgrims (their vehicles or backpacks adorned with tell-tale images and flowers). Evidence of human life becomes scarce while inversely the raw beauty and power of nature grows overwhelming. Altitude thins the air; we pull on sweaters and roll up the car windows against its breathtaking chill.

As we climb the mountain heights, inching toward Juquila, a frosty, white cloud of mist settles over the road. Nothing is visible beyond the stretch of gray pavement just before our eyes. My husband slows the pace of his driving, and our restless children grow quiet in the back seat. We cannot see the red cliffs beyond the road but we know with uncomfortable certainty that—just beyond the curtains of mist—they plunge in a sheer vertical drop. Soft and white as unpicked cotton, the mist hovers ahead of us, opaque and impenetrable, but when we drive *into* it, its texture turns sheer and fine. Native Oaxacans call this area of the Sierra *ñuñuma*, "the land of mists," and I am reminded of the Celtic "thin place" where a veil is said to separate this world from the next.

✳ ✳ ✳ ✳ ✳

In their classic book *Image and Pilgrimage in Christian Culture*, anthropologists Victor and Edith Turner observe that pilgrimage is making a dramatic resurgence in all the world religions. Numbers of visitors at major shrines are increasing—rather than decreasing, as one would suppose, given our assumptions about secularization in the modern world. Pilgrims across the globe leave their ordinary lives in order to voluntarily risk ordeals that will, they hope, lead them to a deeper, more interiorized grasp of religious values at their most basic level. Pilgrims travel from the mundane center of their ordinary lives to a "sacred periphery"—undertaking, in the process, a purifying journey that requires them to leave behind comfort and security in order to reach their destination.

For Christians, the underlying paradigm for pilgrimage is Jesus' Way of the Cross. Sacrifices are to be expected—or even *sought*—as one embarks on the pilgrim's path. In past centuries, Christian pilgrimage was closely associated with penance: monastics could make interior journeys, but ordinary people had to exteriorize their salvific trek through pilgrimage. The pilgrimage *par excellence* was a trip to the Holy Land where one could literally follow the Way of the Cross. When wars made such travels impossible during the Middle Ages, local sites became ready substitutes.[2]

An individual pilgrimage often originated with a vow to God or a saint, promising the trip as an offering for the favor being asked for or having been received. Confronting the perils of the journey was considered both penance and proof, testimony that God, the Virgin Mary, or the saint would not only grant prayers but also protect those along the pilgrim way. This tradition continues in Juquila: either an individual or a family with a personal motivation for making the pilgrimage becomes the catalyst for convincing others to set off on the journey. *Romeros* (pilgrims) urge one another to accept hardships along the way as a sign of their faith; the Virgin will see and alleviate their suffering. (A pilgrim with insufficient faith, on the other hand, is sure to meet misfortune. One woman related that she had resisted her husband's wish to make the pilgrimage; she ended up with a sprained ankle and bloody knees.) Pilgrims repeatedly affirm that the Virgin gives them strength to be able to finish their journey.

Once it is understood that pilgrimage is *supposed to be* difficult, the treacherous roads to Juquila make sense. Not in spite of but rather *because of* its remote location, Juquila serves as an ideal destination for pilgrims. As one realized that pilgrimage inherently implies fervor and courage as well as piety, one can understand why pilgrims voluntarily choose to magnify the arduous nature of the journey by walking or bicycling. Walking pilgrims have been known to walk three, five, ten days or more on exhausting climbs through these impossible mountains; and bicycling here is so grueling that I have seen adventure tourism companies include this route in itineraries for survival sports.

Bicycle pilgrims to Juquila are comprised of the demographic group *least* likely to be found in the pews of a church: young men between fifteen and thirty years old. In one town, eleven male members of a bicyclists' club annually recruit up to 250 young people to make the excursion, setting out on the first Friday of every January. Walking pilgrimages also attract a new generation of pilgrims; a town close to Juquila sends 500 young men and women on a three-day walk each December.

The Turners write, "[T]here is something inveterately populist, anarchical, even anticlerical about pilgrimages in their very essence . . . Pilgrimages are an expression of the *communitas* dimension of any society, the spontaneity of interrelatedness, the spirit which bloweth where it listeth."[3] It might seem that the risks and hardships involved would deter all but the most fervent devotees, but, ironically, the voluntary nature of undertaking a sacred journey makes pilgrimage appealing even to those who might not otherwise be considered normative believers.

One year, a man who is a nurse at my husband's clinic organized a pilgrimage group. In no way resembling the stereotypical image of a pious person, this young man is in his early twenties, flirtatious, somewhat unreliable at work, and sufficiently charismatic to persuade twenty peers to make the trip. He had promised the Virgin that he would organize pilgrimages for three consecutive years if his daughter were born without complications. He is not, however, married to the child's mother!

The group of young men—not regular church-goers—arranged for their parish priest to say Mass for them at midnight just before they left on their trip. Their spirit of adventure was positively contagious. They planned to bike several hours to another church that would host them, but after that, they would be on their own on the open road, resting or sleeping whenever and wherever exhaustion overtook them. A car would follow with food and water, slowly trailing the bicyclists as they inched their way up into the mountains.[4]

Something in the experience of pilgrimage itself opens the believer to an encounter with the Divine Mystery in a new way—as if the physical hardships of the ordeal wear down personal resistance, heightening sensory perception and making the individual more receptive to communication with the Holy. For the young and for those who seek direct, personal contact with God, pilgrimage can be a medium through which an external religious worldview is internalized. Listening to young people describe their insights (radical dependency on God, the beauty of creation, realization of their place in the universe, and wonder at the miracle of their own lives), I have wondered if any number of years of catechesis can equal one night spent in the mountains under the stars on the road to Juquila.

A pilgrim group sets out as a "confluence of innumerable individual woes and hopes"[5] yet becomes more than a sum of individual experiences: the trip tends to bring pilgrims together, even though they may have very different reasons for embarking on the same path. Class distinctions blur in the camaraderie of the journey and the pursuit of a common path. One notable characteristic that pilgrims to Juquila share with their counterparts to other pilgrimage sites in Mexico is that they identify closely with their home village, town, or city.

Pilgrims on the road to Juquila

Most delegations carry banners or wear t-shirts announcing their community of origin. In this way they turn into envoys, representatives, as it were, of the place from which they come. The tiniest rural village can be made visible in the public domain when its name is proudly announced on a banner hung from a vehicle or printed on the back of t-shirts so as to be seen by passersby along the road.

My research on the Juquila devotion (about which little is recorded) was aided immeasurably by a slim volume of poems, songs, miracle stories, and history collected by Juquila resident Juan Castro Méndez, who is also a poet and musician. [6] He writes that, in the longest-standing delegation in recent decades, five thousand pilgrims come annually from the town of Huixcolotla in the neighboring state of Puebla. Bicyclists, musicians, and torch-bearers travel in a pilgrimage that has been visiting Juquila for forty years. A complex system of organization names the delegation's leaders, who serve terms of one or three years and who begin preparations for the following year's trip as soon as the pilgrims arrive home.

Juquila draws pilgrims from different geographical areas in many Mexican states, but locally there is a parallel structure, with designated dates set aside for those who practice particular professions. November 30 is set aside for architects, plumbers, and construction workers to render homage and to have a Mass said for their intentions. December 1 belongs to doctors, nurses, biologists, and pharmacists. Tortilla makers and bakers, painters and woodworkers, lawyers and electricians all take their turns during the novena before the Virgin's feast day. The humblest of laborers finds a place in the devotional schedule.

Like the travelers who set out proudly from distinct communities of origin to converge as one assembly in the sanctuary, workers of diverse trades are acknowledged before blending into the crowds amassed for the Virgin's feast day. On the road to Juquila, differentiation heightens pilgrims' identity—but on arrival, they are absorbed so thoroughly into the collective spirit that *communitas* prevails.

But the most numerous and most constant flow of pilgrims who come to give thanks or to seek favors are those for whom vehicles are a regular means of transport: truck or bus drivers, bicycle messengers, vendors, taxi drivers, devotees who have survived accidents, and those who have had to travel in search of work. One of the most common petitions pilgrims bring is that the Virgin help them acquire a vehicle.

Others bring their cars, buses, or bicycles to be blessed. Patroness of those in movement, she protects her devotees from evil, accidents, and even addictions. As in other sanctuaries, alcoholics come to Juquila to make a *juramento*, a vow to forego drinking for a certain time period; I have seen whole chapters of Alcoholics Anonymous make the pilgrimage.

A pilgrim's raw experiences are given meaning not only by his or her overarching religious tradition, but also by the *specific* collective memory attached to a *particular* pilgrimage site. Millions of Catholics profess an admiration for the Mother of God; but only a personal relationship to a localized representation of the Virgin Mary propels believers to undertake a Marian pilgrimage.

For those of us who are seriously interested in the devotion to the Virgin of Juquila, simply knowing that pilgrimage is on the rise all over the globe is not enough. Why has pilgrimage *to Juquila* surged so dramatically in recent years? What is it about *this* virgin that attracts *these* pilgrims? And why would a migrant in New York insist that Juquila captures the spirit of Mexico?

The presence of water sources near pilgrimage sites is so common in Marian apparition stories about the Mother of God that it might be called a universal feature. In Juquila, the Virgin is said to have appeared to indigenous children on top of an agave plant at the mouth of a stream. A time-honored tradition—whose origin extends back before written memory—mandates that upon entering the town, pilgrims stop to take a purifying bath in Juquila's cold, clear river.

Juquila's plentiful supply of water and a corresponding emphasis on the Virgin's abundant graces are often noted by pilgrims. The recent surge in pilgrimage to Juquila raises the question: What might this "universal" feature, the presence of water, mean for pilgrims who come from agricultural villages now being abandoned because of a scarcity of water? In Oaxaca, by necessity I learned to recycle water several times over, using bath water for flushing toilets or laundry rinse water for mopping floors. Water is one of the most pressing ecological and justice issues of our day, and its scarcity provokes life-changing consequences for communities throughout the developing world.

To borrow anthropological terms, "text" and "context" reinterpret each other in a continual circle of meaning. The text (in this case, the statue or even the town of Juquila itself) achieves credibility and vigor from its context: the lived circumstances of the devotion's adherents. Because pilgrimage centers owe their vitality to popular religious practice (as distinguished from official, hierarchically controlled religious beliefs and activities), they spontaneously illustrate levels of intensity between text and context.

Pilgrimage sites often go through cycles of growth and diminishment. When ecclesial authorities clamp down and when more complex, commercially manipulated symbol systems proliferate at a sanctuary, over time the site center will receive fewer and fewer visitors. Inversely, an existing pilgrimage center may be revived by new generations of devotees. Like a key in a lock, when the symbol system is found to match contemporary believers' deep—often unconscious—emotional and spiritual longings in a way that *fits* their lived context, the devotion can suddenly grow exponentially—even though the sanctuary may already be centuries old.

Juan Castro Méndez observes that, every year, the number of pilgrims to the Virgin's sanctuary increases.

After all, pilgrimage sites are places "where miracles once happened, still happen, and may happen again."[7]

✷ ✷ ✷ ✷ ✷

Perhaps it makes sense that the Virgin of Juquila has become a patroness of those who travel since she is a traveler herself. A small, carved wooden statue styled as a representation of the Immaculate Conception, she was brought across the ocean from Spain to the New World to assist the Dominican Order in evangelization. Fray Jordán de Santa Catalina (born Cristóbal Fuentecillas in 1527 in Salamanca) carried her with him through years of travel through these very mountains. The fact that she is lightweight and small in stature (only a foot tall) made her particularly suitable as a missionary statue. The Virgin went from village to village visiting diverse indigenous communities, transported by mule or—going to places where even a mule could not travel—carried by people on foot.

Fray Jordán crisscrossed these mountains relentlessly, armed with a crucifix and the statue of the Virgin, and I wonder if these sacramentals communicated his message better than his sermons. Fray Jordán did eventually learn Zapotec and achieved an impressive level of fluency, but Zapotec—though dominant—was still only one of many linguistic groups in southern Mexico. Furthermore, the use of indigenous languages itself proved problematic in that native speech simply did not have words for Christianity's key concepts. As in most of New Spain, catechesis had to be done through analogous (as opposed to literal) translation and through non-verbal instruction, including visual representations. The image of a Mother who refused to abandon her Son even at the foot of his cross would be Oaxaca's first—and most perduring—window into Christianity.[8]

As a Spaniard (Spain positioned itself as the defender of the church in the post-Trent era, and the cult of the Virgin Mary delineated boundaries between Catholicism and Protestantism) and a Dominican (the order that has historically championed the rosary), Fray Jordán himself was, not surprisingly, predisposed to a strong Marian devotion. Orphaned at an early age, he was raised by a poor, pious grandmother who prayed the rosary daily, fingering a cord of knots. The depiction of their extreme economic state may be hagiography—one biography tells of his going door-to-door to beg for bread as a child—but the record of Fuentecillas's various apprenticeships under several employers and patrons indicates the family was not well-off. At twenty years of age, Fuentecillas joined the Dominicans, making his profession on September 8 (the feast of the Nativity of Mary), 1548. Ordained a priest in 1552, he said his first Mass already knowing that he would be sent by his superiors to Oaxaca.

Priest-historian José Antonio Gay, in *Historias de Oaxaca* (*Histories of Oaxaca*), relates that one year, severe drought threatened the seasonal harvest. Fray Jordán entered the church, fell on his knees before the altar, and prayed out loud with such fervor and anguish that indigenous onlookers were astonished. Closing his prayer by asking for rain, the Dominican rose and began to say Mass. Before the liturgy had ended, torrents of rain began to fall.

Two key elements of the story reveal, first, the friar's concern for the temporal needs of villagers who were utterly dependent on seasonal precipitation, and second, his efficacy as an intercessor. What interests me about the story is that precisely these two elements have survived through the centuries to become the two pillars of devotion to the Virgin of Juquila. Attributed in the story to the friar, the memory of solicitous care and miraculous power would migrate to her image.

Contemporary pilgrims flock to Juquila because they believe that the Virgin seated there will work miracles for those who need them.

Fray Jordán died in 1592, and before retiring from his itinerant ministry in the Sierras, the Dominican bequeathed his carved image to his indigenous assistant. Thus, toward the end of the sixteenth century, the traveling Virgin took up residence in a straw hut in the village of Amialtepec near Juquila. Indigenous Christians began to walk to Amialtepec on pilgrimage to visit the Virgin. She had sought them, arriving at their isolated communities; now they came to seek her.

And they keep coming.

*   *   *   *   *

Made up of 570 municipalities—the highest number in the Republic —the state of Oaxaca is formed by eight regions, each claiming its own distinct history and local traditions (due in large part to the challenging topography). With Guerrero and Chiapas one of Mexico's three poorest states, Oaxaca lags behind the rest of the country in terms of economic development. The capital city's wealthy, colonial downtown gets 80 percent of its income from tourism, but outside of the capital district—even within the metropolitan area—poverty is prevalent.

On the positive side, precisely because of its isolation, Oaxaca has been able to preserve its cultural and ecological diversity, its "patrimony." Visitors delight in excursions to nearby villages to shop for woven rugs, painted wooden animals (*alebrijes*), green, black, or multi-colored painted or glazed pottery, leather work, mescal liquor, and various styles of traditional dress.

Not all the tourists are foreign. A popular destination for Mexican vacationers who enjoy traditional handcrafts and cuisine, Oaxaca is a place where one can still find handmade (not factory-produced) tortillas made of locally-grown native corn (i.e., not genetically-modified) cooked the old-fashioned way, over wood fires. (The symbolic and culinary importance of cooking with wood was brought home to me when friends explained how their grandmothers used specific types of wood for designated foods, for instance, mesquite for beans, oak for beef.) When McDonald's appeared in Oaxaca, a "Slow Foods" campaign was launched to keep fast food chains out of the main plaza.

While Oaxaca's colonial capital markets the state's traditional way of life, Juquila and other villages *embody* it. Santa Catarina Juquila itself is comprised of four neighborhoods and one shantytown (populated by recently arrived inhabitants attracted by work possibilities). Slightly more than half of Juquila's economically active inhabitants (according to the 2005 census, 51 percent) still make a living from farming, animal husbandry, hunting, or fishing. In other words, they belong to a sector that is quickly becoming extinct but that traditionally has formed the backbone of Mexican life: *campesinos*. As Juquila grows—and every indication points to its continued rapid development—one can imagine that tourism services will displace traditional ways of making a living. But in the meantime, Juquila still wears a recognizable face for pilgrims—so familiar, it looks like home.

A newspaper article captured this insight in describing the devotion of a returned migrant paying a visit to Juquila: "He chose that virgin because she watches over a small, humble town similar to his."[9]

When I first traveled to Mexico, in 1989, the majority of the population lived in rural areas. My host, a rural anthropologist, introduced me to her country's panorama by explaining bluntly, "There are two Mexicos: the rural and the urban." Today, seventy-five percent of Mexicans live in cities.

As the threat to a traditional village way of life accelerates, so does the pace of pilgrimage to Juquila. The Free Trade Agreement of 1994 accelerated rural abandonment, with millions of farming families leaving the countryside for cities in Mexico or for the United States. Agricultural states like Puebla, Oaxaca, Veracruz, Morelos, and Chiapas were among the hardest hit. Is it a coincidence that these same states have dramatically increased their numbers of pilgrims to Juquila?

While the emigrant experience offers more opportunities, it also entails a sense of loss. For those who have set out, and for those left behind in dismantled rural communities, a residue of mourning remains. In a ballad, the well-known pop singer Juan Gabriel laments "*el Mexico que se nos fue*," "the Mexico that has gone from us."

The road to Juquila externalizes the exodus journey in reverse. Instead of leaving the country for the city, travelers depart from urban centers for a rural village. Pilgrims come to Juquila with heightened nostalgia, seeking—and finding—a temporary return to the rapidly vanishing world that they, their parents, or perhaps their grandparents knew, to a way of life that is elsewhere being extinguished.

* * * * *

The word "Juquila" is derived from the Nahuatl *Xiuhquila*, literally, "the place of many blue *quelites* (a wild edible plant)," or, more poetically, "the place of lush vegetation." During the rains, which average 845 millimeters a year, frequent landslides reveal the ochre color of the mountain cliffs, but here and there, where the green vegetation subsides, one can glimpse a cap of fertile, black soil. Every arable foot on the slopes is carpeted with corn and coffee plantings.

In spite of rich natural resources, the communities surrounding Juquila are, literally, dirt poor. Urban poverty certainly exists in Oaxaca City; the hillside cave where the Virgin appeared to our neighbors is in a shantytown lacking in basic services where settlers landed in the hope of finding work in the capital. But here, in the Sierras around Juquila, I glimpse the poverty they are trying to escape. Half of Mexico lives below the poverty line, but in rural areas, the figure rises as high as 85 percent. Outlying farms show signs of destitution in these otherwise idyllic surroundings.

As we descend the heights of the Sierras and come into more populated areas, dogs, hens, roosters, cows, horses, and donkeys lazily line the roads. We pass brick ovens and roadside stands where people are selling regional sweets, woven palm hats, or baskets and handbags. Dirt paths leading off the side of the road are taken by children or elderly people who disappear into the forests or down the slopes to collect wood for cooking fires.

The town of Juquila was settled in 1272 by native colonists from the region of the Mixteca (home to what is now the fourth-largest ethnic group in Mexico; in Oaxaca, second to the Zapotecs). The area surrounding Juquila, however, traditionally belonged to the Chatino people, a coastal tribe that migrated farther into the mountains over the course of centuries and whose material culture can be traced back to 400 BCE. Ethnically and linguistically related to the Zapotecs, the Chatinos separated centuries ago from the Zapotec family tree. Their language is notoriously difficult for non-native speakers to learn and earned the Chatinos their name, "people of difficult words."[10]

A crossroads of sorts—named in Nahuatl, settled by Mixtecs on Chatino lands, bordered closely by Triquis, Amuzgos, Mixtecs, coastal Mixtecs, and Zapotecs—Juquila maintained its language and cultural identity during the Conquest. Like most of New Spain, how-ever, its native people were devastated by rubella and smallpox, and some historians grimly calculate that Oaxaca's indigenous nations were reduced to one-tenth of their pre-Conquest populations.

The Sierras played a definitive role in resistance to Spanish domi-nation. As stated succinctly by historian Margarita Dalton, "The mountains in Oaxaca provided refuge for those who did not accept the new regime."[11] Armed revolts by native nations in 1531, 1547, 1570, and 1660 repelled European invaders, leaving the saying to re-verberate through the centuries, "It is better to die on one's feet than live on one's knees."

Another strategy—enacted in these very mountains—was for whole communities to retreat from contact with Europeans, emerging only when conditions of coexistence seemed possible. Thus, some na-tions were able to avoid complete domination under the Spanish. The Mixe people, for example, were never conquered. Many communities were able to preserve their communal rights to lands and forests.

The Spanish invaders soon realized that they would need to co-opt indigenous forms of organization in order to successfully occupy New Spain. Native leaders were enlisted as allies or brutally repressed, with their communities subjected to forced labor. In the religious realm, missionaries destroyed temples in order to build—literally, over their ruins—Christian churches. Stones of razed temples in Mitla and Teotitlán del Valle, for example, were recycled for the construction of churches. All over Mexico, the policy of substitution proved excep-tionally effective in "christening" pilgrimage sites: the Basilica of St. Mary of Guadalupe and the sanctuary of the Lord of Chalma are two examples of native devotional locations that became enormously pop-ular for indigenous Catholics. (Many of the world's great pilgrimage centers—not only Christian ones—were established in the same way on pilgrimage sites belonging to earlier religions.)

Outside of major population centers, in places where clergy were scarce and where indigenous communities were less subject to direct ecclesial control, traditional religious practice in daily life continued. Unlike the Western mentality, which makes a hard distinction be-tween the sacred and the profane or the natural and the supernatural, the native Mesoamerican worldview sees the natural world and the di-vine as interpenetrated. The emphasis is not on the difference be-tween God and a created universe, but, rather, on the various grades of a continuum. The sacred abides in all things—but is more concentrated in certain beings and certain specific places. In Oaxaca's Sierras, for example, mountaintops, caves, and water springs continued to be considered propitious sites at which to offer petitions (*pedimentos*) for fertility, for rain, for a good crop, or for restored health.[12]

Robert Ricard's still-definitive *The Spiritual Conquest of Mexico* concludes, "The general impression one gets . . . is that the clergy was defeated little by little . . ."[13] Buffered from Spanish influence, steeped in traditional native cosmologies, and converted by missionaries who could not hope to adequately supervise *how* the new faith was practiced, isolated communities like Juquila were able to fuse Catholicism with pre-Hispanic beliefs. This process—termed *syncretism* by anthropologists—is being revisited by theologians, who propose another concept: inculturation.

Syncretism means that indigenous religion is covered over by a Catholic veneer, in effect disguising the continuation of traditional native religion. Inculturation, on the other hand, insists that in every location, during every time period, Christianity has taken root in the soil of local culture, becoming an expression of the gospel in a particular temporal setting. In this process, *indigenous Christians* (neither missionaries nor traditional native religious specialists) would be the protagonists of a creative new incarnation of Christianity.

The Chatino name for the Virgin Mary, *Ho'o María*—used to this day by Chatino Catholics—combines the Spanish name for the Mother of God with the traditional prefix for the sacred that is used in native speech for the sun, the earth, the moon, and the spirits of water, wind, and mountains. Chatino patients at the clinic where my husband worked explained that the Virgin is sacred in this same way. Beings are designated *Ho'o* to show that they are alive, holy, and intimately related to the life of the Chatino people.

* * * * *

As the Virgin of Amialtepec's popularity grew, the local priest, purportedly to avoid abuses, decided to remove the statue from the small straw hut of the catechist to whom Fray Jordán had entrusted her image. The name of the priest, Jacinto Escudero, is recorded—but the name of the main protagonist of the story is not. The only thing known about the indigenous missionary to whom the devotion owes its inception is simply that he was a villager who had worked since the time he was a young man with Fray Jordán. The fact that this villager accompanied the Dominican friar in the northern Sierras—Zapotec-speaking territory—leads me to speculate that he probably served as a translator, while the rapid growth of the devotion under his direction makes me surmise that he must have been a charismatic leader.

As Fray Jordán's missionary zeal faded from memory, a surprising revision in the Virgin's story erased his crucial role. The Virgin, it was said—and this is the version that has passed from generation to generation by word of mouth—had not been *brought* from faraway soil by a conquering foreigner; she had *appeared* directly to the indigenous people. The statue, it is commonly emphasized, had been left in the hands of the villagers of Amialtepec by the Mother of God herself.

According to legend, several village children saw an apparition of the Virgin standing on a rock (or in another variation, atop an agave) beside a flowing stream. When the vision ended, the statue was found where she had been standing. Subsequently, the Virgin appeared to numerous other indigenous converts—as if to bequeath the Christian faith to them without Spanish intermediaries. I first heard this persistent myth of the wandering Virgin in New York: a Zapotec woman in Poughkeepsie swore to me that she had seen for herself grains of sand pouring from the statue's tiny sandals when the sacristans changed the Virgin's clothing. Rumors of her apparitions, especially in caves, abound; to this day, adherents still catch sight of her in Amialtepec. Other tales describe her roaming the Sierras at night, a small, magical being seeking the attention of the native peoples whose mountains she has traveled for five centuries.

Sometime around the turn of the seventeenth century, Escudero, overcoming the Chatinos' resistance, forcibly moved the statue from the catechist's home to the village chapel—also a humble structure with a thatched roof, but this one firmly under the priest's jurisdiction. The statue received indigenous pilgrims in its new shrine until a miraculous incident occurred that conveyed the Virgin's fame beyond native circles.

In 1633, during the slash and burn season when farmers clear the land for the next year's pastures and crops, a fire blazed out of control. Amialtepec's inhabitants fled to the crest of a hill, from which they watched the flames devour the straw roofs of their village. Once the blaze died down, the villagers went to salvage what they could of their homes and chapel. They found the statue of the Virgin amidst the ashes standing atop a pile of rubble, her hair singed and her vestments smoking, but otherwise unharmed.

Once news of the miracle spread to the capital, Spanish and Mexican-born Spanish pilgrims ventured out to see the remarkable image for themselves. A formal investigation by authorities from the capital won credibility for the Virgin when it deemed the miracle "authentic." Around this same time period, the mid-seventeenth century, parallel efforts were being undertaken in various parts of the country by Mexican-born Spaniards who believed that establishing native devotions would advance Mexico's national legitimacy (the first written interpretations of the apparitions of the Virgin of Guadalupe, for example, date from 1648 and 1649).

Even as the fire of 1633 won the Virgin of Amialtepec's approbation by the official church—opening the devotion to non-indigenous Catholics—the same incident cemented the native identity of the Virgin: the tiny face of the statue was "darkened" by smoke, making her countenance permanently resemble those of the indigenous people she had come to these lands to claim as her own.

As the Virgin's popularity grew (and clergy became more concerned over control of the devotion), it was decided the statue should be moved to the larger, more prestigious parish seat in Santa Catarina Juquila. So famous a virgin, it was argued, should be housed in a sanctuary more suitable to her status. However, the Virgin didn't seem to agree. The statue kept disappearing at night, only to turn up among the straw huts of Amialtepec. This scenario was repeated numerous times—over the course of several decades! It seemed that neither locks nor security guards could deter the Virgin. In 1719, an episcopal decree was promulgated declaring that the image must remain in Santa Catarina Juquila. (I am always amused by this detail; since when does the Mother of God take orders from a bishop?)

Oral tradition tells the story differently, and according to one version I have heard devotees in Juquila enclosed the statue in a "cell" made of flower petals. Whatever version of the story one accepts, the transition was completed. The Virgin of Amialtepec was rechristened the "Virgin of Juquila," and in 1746 an ambitious reconstruction of Juquila's church was begun—an enormous undertaking for a small Indian town. When it was completed, the new church was celebrated throughout Oaxaca as a magnificent and spacious sanctuary.

Jealously guarded for centuries after the episcopal decree, the Virgin never left the church. In 1769, lightning struck the church but the statue was miraculously unharmed. In 1931, an earthquake shook the region but both the church and the statue survived. In 1999, another earthquake hit, shattering the glass chamber around the statue but leaving it, still standing, on its niche. After this last earthquake, the Virgin left the constraints of her sanctuary. A procession led by the parish priest escorted the Virgin through the streets so that she could see for herself the damage done to the town. The procession helped catalyze the effort to rebuild and, aided by financing and donations provided by devotees, Juquileños repaired the sanctuary and other structures damaged by earthquake.

Today, the church building cannot contain the thousands of pilgrims who come to visit its small Virgin. The sanctuary, once considered majestically vast, seems diminished as crowds of devotees grow. They overflow from the vast doorway of the church into the atrium and spill outside of the atrium gates into the town's main square.

* * * * *

After entering the municipality of Juquila (which measures 811 square kilometers), most pilgrims make a detour of six kilometers before arriving at the center of town and its famous sanctuary. They customarily stop first at the Pedimento—a "popular" religious site without which a visit to the "official" church is considered incomplete. Both geographically and symbolically, the Pedimento comes first.

There are two turn-offs to the Pedimento, and they meet in a fork along a deeply gutted dirt road. Cinderblocks are placed along the edges of the path in an apparent attempt to hold up the soil during the rainy season and to prevent wind erosion. Along the path, vendors sell flowers, religious articles, sandwiches, sodas, and handmade tortillas. Food stands consist of small propane camping stoves or metal drums containing wood fires and are covered by plastic tarps overhead.

Most alluring are the stands selling *ex-votos* (from the Latin for "of the vow" or "of the promise") in the form of tiny peso notes or dollar bills that look like miniature Monopoly money and the *milagritos* (little miracles), small metal objects shaped like objects, people, animals, or body parts to be pinned to the Virgin's veil or robe. The *milagritos* are chosen to represent that for which a petition or thanks is being offered: a book for the student, a heart for love, a leg for a knee

A vendor sells milagritos at a stall along the road to the Pedimento

injury, and so on. Originating in the Mediterranean world under the cult of the Greek god of medicine, it is an ancient European custom that gained new vigor and longevity when transplanted to the fertile ground of native American sensibility.

Victor and Edith Turners might well have been writing about Juquila—especially the Pedimento—when they outlined the trajectory of the development of a pilgrimage site.

> A pilgrimage's foundation is typically marked by visions, miracles, or martyrdoms. The first pilgrims tend to arrive haphazardly, individually and intermittently, though in great numbers, "voting with their feet;" their devotion is fresh and spontaneous. Later, there is progressive routinization . . . of the sacred journey. Pilgrims . . . tend to come in organized groups, in sodalities, confraternities, and parish associations, on specified feast days, or in accordance with a carefully planned calendar. Marketing facilities spring up along the way . . . A whole elaborate system of licenses, permits, and ordinances, governing mercantile transactions, pilgrims' lodgings, and the conduct of fairs, develops as the number of pilgrims grows and

their needs and wants proliferate . . . The pilgrims' Mass itself is
often the climax of an escalating series of devotions held at
auxiliary way stations and subordinate intrabasilican shrines.
To cater to the fired-up pilgrim's spiritual needs, the merchants of holy wares set up booths in the market, where they
sell devotional statuettes and pictures, rosaries, missals, sacred
tracts, and a variety of other sacramental objects . . .[14]

Instead of driving, pilgrims often take the long walk—three kilometers long—to a small chapel at the end of an eroded uphill dirt
road (until recently, when the road was bulldozed, *all* pilgrims had to
walk: this path was impassable by vehicle). The noise and bustle of the
merchants at the foot of the Pedimento fade from hearing as travelers
advance up the slope. From the summit, a stunning panoramic view
of the green valley opens up with the town of Juquila in full view.

It is easy for me to imagine why the Chatino people have historically regarded this hilltop as a holy place. Its mountain air clears the
mind in peace and tranquility. Pilgrims come and go, but a quiet,
meditative atmosphere prevails. Brisk currents from surrounding
alpine forests cool the skin while the sun's rays—intensified by the
high altitude—warm one's face and back. Travelers acknowledge each
other, but converse softly, or not at all. I would like to spend hours
here, lost in thought or prayer or simply resting in the quiet.

The Pedimento's roots stretch into past centuries, when indigenous petitioners made offerings here. Nowadays, the site enjoys new-
found popularity. The chapel's construction is recent, and, judging
from the inscriptions on them, the pews inside the chapel have all
been donated within the last seven years. Outside, conditions are still
quite primitive. For example, the stand in which pilgrims place candles is made of sheets of corrugated metal nailed together to protect
the huddle of flickering flames from the wind.

Approaching the chapel, one passes banners on display along the
walkway, whipping in the wind. These are the banners that had been
hung from the buses or other vehicles on the road to Juquila bearing
the names of the pilgrims' home communities. Occasionally, painted
banners tell through pictures and words of a miracle attributed to the
Virgin's intercession.

Entering the small chapel, the visitor's eye is drawn to a succession of murals painted on the walls and roof. In one painting, Fray

Jordán travels with the diminutive Virgin. In another, indigenous children kneel in front of her apparition beside a stream. In yet another, the Virgin stands atop the pile of rubble in the village of Amialtepec.

Better than any other example, the devotion of Juquila demonstrates the dual character of official and popular religious expressions, for at the Pedimento, on the outskirts of Juquila—in an area even more isolated than the remote sanctuary—a homemade devotion site parallels the clerically controlled pilgrimage center in town. Some twenty years ago, this marginal, traditional offering site outside the town center began to gain importance as a populist counterpoint to Juquila's elaborate sanctuary, as if the devotion were becoming too domesticated and the Virgin's roots in a peripheral indigenous cult had to be reestablished. Just as the Virgin used to travel from the sanctuary in town to the straw huts of Amialtepec, this devotion escapes the confines of Juquila's church walls. Behind the altar of the Pedimento chapel, a white veil hangs draped from a mannequin, a copy of the famous mantle in the main church under which pilgrims pass, and an *alter ego* of the carefully crafted, elaborately adorned, inaccessible Virgin of Juquila stands sturdily on the altar.

Unlike the official Virgin—protected by a glass casement in an elevated niche that cannot be reached—this statue is fully accessible to pilgrim hands. This Virgin wears a mantle onto which visitors easily pin *milagritos*, photos, and money. Her small size, dark color, long hair, and regal vestments simulate those of the original statue. But while the official Virgin looks delicate, exquisite, and dainty, this popular Madonna appears crude and rough. Each time I look at her countenance, I am stunned by its primitive ingenuity.

The Virgin of Juquila is dark: in the words of a popular song, she is *"linda, chiquita y morena"* ("beautiful, small and dark"). If any doubt ever existed about her color, it would be resolved by taking one look at this twin image. To those unfamiliar with her story, the official statue, carved in Europe, might pass as an olive-skinned Spanish virgin, but *this* image, stemming from purely popular expression, portrays the Virgin of Juquila clearly as a Black Madonna.[15] Weathered, implacable, resistant—she is carved from solid wood whose dark grain speaks of the fecund black earth, the fertile power of the feminine, land soaked with water, the black soil on the slopes of Juquila.

Standing before her, I am struck by how much it has taken me to arrive at this moment with five children and a husband in a borrowed pick-up truck, our marriage battered but mercifully intact, our children healthy and reasonably well-turned out. My whole life has led up to this moment, but the journey has taken its toll. I am overcome by weariness, pierced by a sudden awareness of how much it has taken out of me. It's more than the fatigue of a seven-hour trip on bumpy, perilous roads with no decent bathrooms along the highway and carsick kids asking every fifteen minutes, "Are we there yet?" It's all the many roadblocks I encounter along the way in trying to live my one, true life.

As I contemplate the mute statue before me, two Mayan women kneeling in the aisle sing, chant, and pray in Tzotzil, their voices lifting and dipping with intonation, punctuated by the occasional pauses when their silence sinks deeply into the quiet. I note the crafts they carry to sell, the treads of their upturned sandals caked with mud, the ribbons fraying at the ends of their braids. I cannot understand their words but I listen with my heart. In some mysterious way, we share a love for this stump of roughly hewn wood topped by an impossible-looking wig, a figure whose blunt features resemble those of the losing competitor in a boxing match. She is an ancestor we hold in common, a grandmother whose youthful beauty has long since faded, but whose thinned hair, sagging flesh, and gnarled hands make us comfortable in her presence.

The effect is cathartic and strangely purifying.

After paying their respects to the dark Virgin, pilgrims go out to the thin air of the hillside behind the chapel, where a huge, granite cross looms over the slope. It is exactly here that the Pedimento draws believers into its compelling radius. The most essential teaching of Christian theology is distilled into a single stone erected over an indigenous foundation. On mountaintops and at water sources, in native spirituality *pedimentos* were (and are) offered where local people discovered *cruces verdes*: literally "green crosses," trees whose branches grew naturally to intersect in a cruciform. The underlying paradigm of Christ's passion is made visible in the thousands of crosses extending as far as the eye can see.

Even if I were *not* a believer, I would be moved by the sight, for each cross represents a human story of triumph over suffering. According to custom, to make a petition one brings or makes an offering at the foot of the Pedimento cross. After the petition is granted, the supplicant must return, this time to present a smaller cross of his or her own. Fancier creations are made of wrought-iron, humbler versions of unfinished wood.

Crosses line the slopes of the Pedimento as testimonies to favors received

Some are gilded, others are adorned with flowers. Most are inscribed, sometimes with just the words, "*Gracias, Virgencita,*" "Thank you, dear Virgin." Planted like stakes into the ground or hung from the branches of trees, all the way down the hillside, crosses clutter the green landscape. Occasionally swept up in piles to make room for new ones, the crosses remind pilgrims of the waves of grateful believers who have returned here before them.

The cross symbolizes not only favors received but also the testimony of a safe passage. As expressed in the messages writ-

A cross thanks the Virgin of Juquila for her intercession

ten on banners or crosses, the fact of simply having made the perilous trip requires gratitude. The grace received on the road is the same grace conferred at its destination. In one of the deepest truths of spiritual life, just being given the strength to undertake life's journey—which inevitably must entail suffering—is enough.

But the Pedimento's main purpose is to provide a setting for pilgrims to make petitions related to temporal needs. The ochre clay of the hillside is shaped by millions of hands forming representations of the favors they have come to ask for. Not surprisingly, the most popular petitions relate to vehicles. Below the cross a wooden table is set out where pilgrims can work at fashioning figures, cars, trucks, buses, animals, and houses made from mud scooped out of clay pockets in the Pedimento slopes. On one trip, we met a Nahuatl-speaking family from Guerrero who fashioned a two-story house—complete with vehicles and horses in the yard and babies on a clay balcony.

Petitions such as these tend to make us First World Christians of the dominant culture cringe. After all, we reason, prayers cannot build a house; in the same situation, we avail ourselves of credit banking and real estate agencies. And fertility, we believe, is a medical—not a religious—matter.

Clay figurines representing pilgrims' petitions at the Pedimento

I was reminded of the vast difference between scientific and non-scientific worldviews by a story I heard recently from another family, also from Guerrero. One year, severe drought in their area was followed by torrents of rain. The parched land could not absorb the precipitation and run-off resulted. Rain and flooding continued for days on end, damaging houses and crops and inundating roads. My scientific worldview immediately identified the problem as climactic changes combined with a local lack of adequate infrastructure (drainage pipes, retaining walls, etc.). The villagers involved, while not disagreeing with these as *factors* of the crisis, saw the underlying *cause* as a religious-spiritual one: fundamentalist Protestant sects have made inroads in this area in recent years. Both Catholics and Protestants saw the floods as divine retribution—against Catholics for refusing to be saved or, conversely, against Protestants for abandoning the true faith!

A scientific worldview finds this interpretation ludicrously irrelevant, but to the villagers, it explains the mysterious *causative* dimension of a given situation, not just its visible symptoms. Both views consider the floods a rupture in the harmony or balance of the natural ecosystem—but for the villagers, the ecosystem includes an invisible, sacred dimension that sets chains of events in motion. Their way of thinking addresses existential questions familiar to any group of people who have found themselves in dire straits: *Why us? Why now?*

The Nahua family we met at the Pedimento did not expect the Virgin to supply them a ready-made house but, rather, to facilitate their efforts to build it themselves. They have been setting aside construction materials bought little by little with money earned in the United States. Given the Virgin's intercession, *if* it is God's will (a commonly repeated caveat), the project will go smoothly, that is, uninterrupted by any number of the unforeseen circumstances that complicate the lives of poor people. In seeking the Virgin's help as an ally—a powerful advocate capable of working miracles on their behalf—they draw on a pre-existing kinship relationship. Since she is their mother, she will take their request to heart. The petition will be heard because of this relationship, or in popular religious language, their *faith*.

In turn, the family promises to return on pilgrimage to give thanks, depositing their cross along with the thousands of others. True to the theology of grace (which is a gift, not earned), the Virgin hears them not because they *deserve* her favor, but because God may deem to confer it, through her intercession; they *seek* it. The interactive devotional customs of Juquila are founded on the primordial cardinal virtue that governs *campesino* life, the natural law from which no villager can escape, the unbending rule of reciprocity. Being in relationship is not limited to sentimental feelings—although an emotional element is definitely involved—but entails a pragmatic give-and-take that gets each of us through life, together.

Contemporary detractors of the Juquila devotion complain that many pilgrims come driven by superstition, seeking material gains. They echo the Turners, who warn that devotions can become "instruments by which to obtain material goals" instead of "salvation from the material order." Popular practices should be "lenses bringing into focus" the essential insights of faith, making the heart of doctrine accessible to the people at large—but instead can become "blinders."[16]

The Juquila devotion slips easily into *fanaticismo,* "fanaticism," with its exaggerated legends about the Virgin. In the past, Juquileños dressed the small statue in red vestments—until they realized that this caused traffic accidents and made bulls in the vicinity grow restless. Worse, the Virgin is said to be *sentida* (touchy) and even *vengativa* (vengeful). A rock formation outside town, legend tells, is actually two petrified pilgrims punished by the Virgin for adultery while on the road to Juquila.

A friend's father, who owned a trucking fleet, was a long-time benefactor of the sanctuary at Juquila. He used to bring his family on the Virgin's feast day each year, making a stop afterward at the shore. When the children of this family anticipated the excursion to the beach more eagerly than the visit to the sanctuary, complaining about having to stop at the church, accidents began to happen to their father's trucks. The owner began to schedule his family's two trips separately, and the accidents stopped.

Understandably, some pastoral ministers are offended by their perception that Mary is being treated as God, working miracles and granting favors, rather than as a saint who intercedes with God on our behalf. They are uncertain about how the devotion fits within its larger Christian context, especially regarding justice issues. It has been said that even narco-traffickers claim the Virgin's intercession. In seeking a vertical relationship to solve their immediate needs, pilgrims may lose a sense of social responsibility—and with it, the potential to achieve structural change. (One priest I know prepares his delegation by asking pilgrims to make a retreat together in which they identify as a group their personal and collective petitions as a parish.)

Another common concern is devotees' tendency to lose sight of the Virgin of Juquila as the biblical Mary of Nazareth, and the statue as one image among many representations of the Mother of God. Yet, the Virgin of Juquila, known affectionately as *la Juquilita* ("little Juquila"), draws on centuries of established Marian tradition precisely through the trademark that has most endeared her to devotees. The Virgin of Juquila's distinctive feature, a long white veil, extends from her statue encased high above the main altar of the parish church and is draped over a passageway constructed behind the altar at the top of a flight of stairs—so that one can actually pass under her mantle.

* * * * *

One of the earliest known images of the Virgin Mary from antiquity shows a *Madonna Orante*, a veiled woman praying with upraised hands. As women traditionally wore head coverings in the ancient world, it is not surprising that Mary was portrayed as veiled. Christianity, after all, started off as an Eastern religion—a shoot of Judaism planted in pagan soil, flourishing first in Asia Minor and Northern Africa where many women even today use head coverings. What *does* intrigue me is the question of how the Virgin's veil has traveled across continents and through the centuries, coming to rest on the miniature crown and little shoulders of the Virgin of Juquila.

In legend, at the moment when she is being taken into heaven during the Assumption, the Virgin Mary quickly unfastens her sash and hands it to St. Thomas the Apostle. Throughout the centuries, diverse traditions have inspired faith in believers regarding miraculous garments worn by the Virgin Mary.[17]

The *Maphorion*, or Holy Veil, follows this mythical trajectory. A piece of cloth believed to have been worn by the Virgin Mary during her lifetime, it was kept in a transparent glass receptacle in Constantinople's Church of the Holy Case. Legend relates that the veil was carried from Jerusalem during the reign of Leon I (457–474 CE). The intercession of the Mother of God was made visible in the mantle that provided safety and refuge. Protecting the city's inhabitants against invaders, plagues, earthquakes, and civil war, the Virgin of the Veil was given the title *Episkeupsis*, "Protection."

On July 2, the feast day of the Virgin of the Holy Veil, the emperor would take a ritual bath in water springing from the hands of a marble veiled *Madonna Orante*. One ancient hymn includes these words: "With your venerated veil, O Immaculate One, you cover the whole heavens clothed with clouds. By venerating it with faith, we glorify You, O refuge of our souls!" A prayer from the lectionary reads: "To all the faithful, as a vestment of incorruptibility, you have given your holy clothing which protects your holy body, O you who are the divine shelter of men."

Devotion to Mary's Holy Veil finds its most eloquent expression in the popular retelling of a foundational miracle story. In the tenth century, St. Andrew the Fool beheld a vision of the *Theotokos* (Mother of God) escorted into the Church of the Holy Case by St. John the Baptist and other saints. The Virgin knelt down and prayed, then, taking hold of her veil, extended it over the people in the church.

The Eastern Church's representation of the Virgin Mary of the Veil migrated west, probably with the Crusaders, as the Mother of Mercy, *La Madonna della Misericordia*. The earliest depiction I know of dates from the first third of the fourteenth century and is a work by Italian artist Niccolo di Segna. This form of religious art began to proliferate in fifteenth-century Europe with portrayals of Mary's garment adapted to its new setting. As Marian writer Sally Cunneen explains, "European artists transformed the veil into something more understandable to Western viewers."

In an altarpiece by Piero della Francesca (mid-fifteenth-century Italy) a blond Mother of Mercy extends her generous mantle over miniature-sized prominent local citizens. The protective garment is no longer a veil but a cloak, and the Virgin's head is uncovered. A more appealing representation, painted by the Provencal artist Jean Miralhet (c. 1442), depicts the Mother of Mercy and the people of Nice. The Virgin spreads her mantle, which begins as a hood covering the crown of her own head and then drapes down to envelop her constituents in its tender sweep.

Noticeable in both the Eastern and Western traditions of the veil is the *collective* nature of the Virgin's protection. The Eastern Virgin of the Veil was understood to exercise her role for the whole Byzantine Empire, and European representations of the Mother of Mercy typically place entire communities under her care. Surely one of the key aspects of Marian spirituality is the way in which images of her evoke deeply personal associations of nurturing while at the same time tapping into shared human experiences.

In Mexico, a commonly recited children's prayer (our own children said it every morning at their Catholic school) expressly calls upon Mary in her role as a protective intercessor. Since this prayer makes mention of the Virgin's mantle, it is often recited to the Virgin of Juquila. Note the sudden shift from first person singular to plural:

> Sweet Mother, stay near, do not turn your gaze away. Accompany me wherever I go and never leave me. Since you protect us as our true Mother, cover us with your mantle, and have the Father, Son and Holy Spirit bless us.[18]

Like the devotion to the Niño Dios (represented by statues of the baby Jesus which are cradled and rocked during the Christmas season), the Niño de Atoche (a slightly older version of the Christ Child), or other less-than-full-size representations of Mary, the Virgin of Juquila's miniature size endears her to devotees. As an image of the Immaculate Conception, her small stature suits her well: chosen as God's favorite daughter to someday become the Mother of Christ, this image of Mary is considered precious, exquisite, and whimsical as a child. The lyrics of a traditional Guadalupan hymn, "*La Paloma Blanca*" ("The White Dove"), are often employed in honor of the diminutive, immaculate virgin.

Other songs and prayers have been composed explicitly for the Virgin of Juquila. The following unpolished and popular version can be found reprinted in newspapers, left scrawled on scraps of paper in churches, or—incongruous as it may seem—posted hundreds of times on the Internet:

> Dear Mother, Virgin of Juquila, Virgin of our hope, our life is yours. Protect us from all evil. In this world of injustice, misery and sinfulness, if you see our lives being disturbed, do not abandon us, dear Mother. Protect pilgrims and accom-

pany us on all our journeys. Watch over the poor who go hungry; as for the bread which is taken from them, restore it to them. Accompany us throughout our lives and free us from sin.[19]

While its history extends back to the *Maphorion*, the Virgin of Juquila's veil owes its extraordinary contemporary vitality to the Mexican adaptation of the Spanish *rebozo* (traditional women's shawl). Like the *cruces verdes* (tree branch crosses) that predate the cross at the Pedimento or the *milagritos* that proved so compatible with native spirituality, the veil of the Virgin Mary, having migrated successfully to Europe where it made its way into religious art, found a new incarnation in the traditional women's shawl in New Spain. I would even say that the *rebozo* defines the practice of pilgrims passing under the Virgin of Juquila's mantle.

A definitively female garment that cuts across social and ethnic differences, *rebozos* can be found all over Latin America. But they are *most* functional for *rural* women—even more, for rural *mothers*. The typical image of an indigenous woman depicts a mother with her child wrapped in a shawl across her back—a sight still commonplace in Oaxaca.

A young Mexican-American friend from the Bronx went to Mexico for the first time to visit her father's village in Puebla. Toward the end of her stay, she bought a *rebozo*, explaining that for her it represented a reminder of her family's way of life and the preciousness of her inheritance.

Eminently practical, a shawl has many uses for women still living in traditional settings. Its most obvious purpose is to shelter its wearer from cold, dust, or the sun. It can be used to carry vegetables from the market, or to hold gathered wild flowers, plants, or herbs. It comes in handy for sitting on so as not to dirty one's dress, to cover one's head at church, or to spread on the ground when embracing a lover. Above all, a *rebozo* is used to cover a sleeping baby or to carry small children—especially while traveling.

Cradled in the warmth of the mother's body, a baby can nurse to sleep in comfort. The sounds and sights of the outside world are muffled by the fabric in which the child is enveloped. Pressed against the mother's skin with its reassuring scent, the vulnerable crown of his or her head covered, a baby can be carried for hours. Really expert *rebozo* wearers can wrap an infant with no knots—just folds, skillfully wrapped to make the baby's weight itself secure the arrangement, leaving the mother's two hands free for other tasks. Older babies are tied onto a mother's front or back, thus allowing her to move with more speed and surety. Yet another way mothers use the *rebozo* is to tie it around the torso of toddlers learning to walk and, in this way, keeping their children from falling while at the same time encouraging them to take their own, first steps.

* * * * *

As we approach the town of Juquila, the greenery of lush vegetation proliferates right up to the town's entrance—as if the land doesn't know yet that it has been urbanized. Signs for showers and bathrooms lettered crudely on scraps of wood hang on the equally crude unfinished cinderblock or corrugated metal walls of the facilities they advertise. Many pilgrims choose to walk the six kilometers from the Pedimento to the parish church as a culmination of their pilgrimage. I have seen some do so barefoot.

According to what friends have told us, in the past, during the rainy season, Juquila's roads would often become impassable. Vehicles that chanced the trip often got stuck in the mud, their unfortunate passengers depending on the next vehicle to pull them out. During the dry season, pilgrims would arrive at the town covered in dust from head to foot, their scalps coated with a cap of fine, red soot. Nowadays these roads—paved within the past fifteen years—cannot contain the heavy flow of cars, buses and vans that arrive for the Virgin's feast day. In December, the streets in town are closed to vehicular traffic in order to prevent chaos.

In terms of area, the downtown appears surprisingly small, basically made up of the market and the plaza, on which the municipal offices and the church sit heavily. Each time we drive in, I am unnerved by the steepness of the main thoroughfare that circles the small center of town. From every vantage point in Juquila, the church that houses the famous virgin can be seen to cut a majestic figure against the backdrop of broad, verdant mountains. The sanctuary's imposing presence dominates the town—its economy, its landscape, its people.

The sanctuary of the Virgin of Juquila, Santa Catarina Juquila

The 2005 update on Mexico's National Census lists 14,380 inhabitants in Juquila's municipality as a whole, with eighty percent of its 2,715 homes having access to potable water and electricity. A more descriptive inventory, taken from Castro Méndez's work published in the year 2000, gives readers a better idea of the provincial character of Juquila. The entire municipality claims two pre-schools, two primary schools, one secondary school and one high school; a bustling central market which caters to pilgrims; a small regional hospital; three pharmacies and two private doctors; a folkloric dance group and traditional orchestra; two bus stations; two public phones and one telegraph office; twenty-five hotels, twenty restaurants, seventy taxis, and innumerable stands and ambulatory vendors. Another attraction deserves mention: a dancing stallion whose owner demonstrates horse and rider's talents regularly on the main plaza.

On our first trip, we found the town's single bank machine and the only really nice restaurant-hotel along a short strip of newly constructed, garishly painted concrete buildings. On subsequent trips, we stayed with the family of one of a handful of students who set out from Juquila to pursue university studies in the capital.

When finally arriving at the very center of Juquila, I was struck by the realization that, while immigrant friends in New York had described the town in detail, they had omitted one essential factor: its obvious indigenous character. The town of Juquila looks like a Spanish plaza superimposed on an Indian village. Browsing through the marketplace or lingering in the church atrium, I could overhear diverse indigenous languages and observe many styles of traditional dress.

Juquila attracts native American pilgrims from all over southern Mexico. Besides Chatinos, on our trips we met a busload of Nahuatl speakers from Puebla; the family from Guerrero, also Nahuas; a delegation of Zapotecs traveling by caravan from Guelatao (Benito Juarez's birthplace in Oaxaca's Sierra Norte); and a host of Mayan vendors from Chiapas.

Oaxaca has been called Mexico's "quintessential" indigenous state by intellectuals. Other states such as Chiapas, Yucatán, and Hidalgo also have high percentages of indigenous inhabitants, and in terms of sheer numbers, Mexico City—a sprawling monster of some 28 million inhabitants—holds first place. But Oaxaca claims the most ethnicities, in other words, Native American nations that maintain their distinct identities: sixteen ethno-linguistic indigenous nations and two ethnic groups. According to Mexico's 2000 census, 37 percent of the people in the state speak a native language as their first language. Still, according to anthropologists, if other factors are taken into consideration, fully 70 percent of the state's population can be identified as indigenous. Approximately 10,500 communities preserve languages, customs, and worldviews rooted in their own cultures.

Both intensely heterogeneous—given its many different ethnic groups—and overwhelmingly indigenous, Oaxaca, then, makes an ideal location for the salvation of native souls.

But Mexico lives uneasily in its Indian skin.

National policies dating from the 1920s have encouraged Mexicans to see themselves exclusively as *mestizos*, that is, originating from a mixture of Spanish and native American bloodlines—while ignoring the reality of indigenous nations that retain their own identities. Children speaking traditional languages in school were punished, and Mexico's glorious Indian past was lauded while simultaneously being relegated to just that: the past. The word *indio* in common parlance still designates a person as "backward."

In the Zapatista uprising of 1994, Mayans in Chiapas exposed their resistance to the signing of the Free Trade Agreement, shocking the Mexican national conscience with the realization that, not only did indigenous nations still exist but they had been "written out" of the country's future.

Mexico's deep-seated ambivalence about indigenous identity explains why its cultural patrimony (as measured by native languages or other explicit indicators of ethnicity) is being lost at an alarming rate—even as demographics based on DNA show that the population's number of genetically "indigenous" inhabitants will soon reach the level believed to have been reached before the Conquest.

A couple living in the capital who became our children's godparents (our *compadres*) come from a coastal Mixtec town which predates the Conquest. During the early months of our friendship, when we asked if they spoke "dialect," they quickly replied that they did not (a stigma is attached to indigenous language in the capital). It was not until we visited their town that we learned that our *compadre*'s family speaks Mixtec at home; the husband's grandmother, a weaver, wears the traditional purple and burgundy striped skirt of the area's native women, and all political, social, economic, and religious discourse in the town is bilingual. When our children, after visits to their godparents, began to punctuate their Spanish with Mixtec, my husband and I joked that our *compadres* had "learned" a lot of Mixtec in a short time.

Because Juquila's discourse is religious, it appeals to popular sentiment stemming from indigenous sensibilities while at the same time allowing pilgrims to sidestep thorny issues of ethnicity by identifying themselves through their communities of origin. Pilgrimage to Juquila is satisfying because it touches the heart and soul of indigenous Catholic spirituality. Mexico's *mestizo* veneer cannot completely hide its indigenous cultural identity especially that of the southern states from which the majority of Juquila's pilgrims originate. Pilgrims to Juquila come seeking an encounter with a Virgin who understands them . . . who *belongs* to them.

In a custom that has been discontinued in recent times, once a year, on her feast day, the Juquilita's glittering, miniature image—darkened by candle smoke and stained from sporadic contact with human hands, used to be lowered delicately from the lofty niche to the sanctuary floor, to be kissed and caressed by her faithful.

* * * * *

With its geography isolating the town from the rest of the country (and even from Oaxaca's urban centers), Juquila participated only marginally in the war for independence from Spain. Its isolation was unhappily ended by the introduction of an export crop. Too mountainous for large-scale agriculture of other crops, the land around Juquila—with its combination of rich soil, high altitude, and cool climate—proved exceptionally suited for the growing of coffee. Investors came from outside the municipality to start plantations, and Chatinos became day laborers on their own land.

Constant agrarian conflicts mark this period, with three Chatino uprisings during the last quarter of the nineteenth century. While still somewhat removed from the convulsions of the rest of the country, Juquileños sympathized with another indigenous small farmer, Emiliano Zapata, during the 1910 Revolution.

But the benefits of the Revolution never really reached Juquila. In most of rural Mexico, the old *cacique* system of local strong-arm leaders simply combined with a new, electoral one. Political offices passed from one member of the local governing family to another. In Oaxaca, agrarian reform was achieved on only a limited scale—as evidenced by the small, family-owned coffee farms in outlying areas of Juquila's municipality.

Recent heightened interest in Juquila's famous Virgin has brought new resources to the region. One wonders whether, in time, Juquila's very success will undermine the rural identity which its pilgrims so prize. On a legal-political level, this transformation has already happened: in January 2006—in spite of the fact that its population size does not qualify Juquila as an urban center—the town was elevated to the status of a city in order to facilitate the development of services for increasing numbers of pilgrims.

Taking at face value Castro Mendez's figures and comparing them to the census update, it would appear that the town of Juquila's population has more than doubled—in just five years! Furthermore, a notable shift has taken place in the proportion of Juquila's native to non-Chatino inhabitants. The town has changed from being more than two-thirds Chatino-speaking to less than one-third. The consequences of social stress inherent in these rapid cultural changes remain to be seen.

The hotel-restaurant where we ate on our first day in Juquila had been bought by a couple from Puebla; the wife explained that her husband is in New York City, working to save up the capital needed to get their new business off the ground. Her son, not being Oaxacan—much less Juquileño—has had a hard time making friends in school. She complained that the pilgrims have faith, but that Juquileños don't—for them, the Virgin is "good for business."

On the other hand, our young friend the university student, whose family has been Juquileño for generations, scoffs at the newcomers. They displace Juquila's rightful owners, she claimed, by buying up property and businesses. She points out the few stores and hotels around the plaza that are still Juquileño-owned.

To further complicate matters, other Juquileños—those of humbler backgrounds—insinuate that the non-Chatino, business-owning families around the plaza (like that of our university friend) come from *cacique* families who use Juquila's development to serve their own political and economic interests.

Centuries ago, the principal power struggle in Juquila's nascent devotion was played out in the rivalry between Fr. Escudero and the anonymous Chatino catechist. Later, in the tug-of-war between villagers of Amialtepec and their town-residing neighbors, the Virgin "disappeared" from the parish seat and "re-appeared" in straw huts. Today, Juquila's bitter political disputes, generated in large part by frictions caused by the devotion's growth, have become a source of shameful notoriety.

As Juquila's popularity grows, so do tensions regarding the town's development. Accommodating droves of pilgrims in such a small town calls for a dramatic expansion of local infrastructure. Renovations, paving projects, and new construction all require municipal authorization, as do the issuance of permits and licenses for hotels, restaurants, taxis, booths, and stores. For twenty years, differences regarding legislation and implementation of public policies have repeatedly erupted in violence. The single most contentious issue? Control of the Pedimento.

Millions of pesos annually change hands at the populist pilgrimage site. This is income that is not managed by the church, but by local authorities. With revenues unaccounted for and corruption rampant, tensions escalate, and political divisions cause feuds among Juquileños who are caught up in the struggle over the Pedimento.

The sleepy, picturesque plaza and quaint church seem an unlikely setting for shoot-outs, clergy kidnappings, and tear gas. But, with its heightened profile as a potential gold-mine for tourism and its complicated local politics, Santa Catarina Juquila has become the stage for a tragedy. In 1993, seven members or sympathizers of the opposition party (*el Partido de la Revolución Democrática*, the Democratic Revolutionary Party, known commonly by its acronym, PRD) were killed. Community leaders pointed to the political party that has controlled Oaxaca since 1929, the *Partido Revolucionario Institucional* (Party of the Institutional Revolution, or the PRI).

More recently, *el Movimiento Ciudadano Juquileño* (The Juquila Citizens' Movement) was formed. Comprised of PRD members along with members of the right-wing *Partido para Acción Nacional* (Party for National Action), it also includes a reformist faction of the PRI. The movement's common goal was to challenge the mainline PRI in upcoming municipal elections. After results were announced, tensions erupted, along with accusations of vote buying and fraud. Protestors held marches and, for a short time, took over the municipal offices next to the church. In one particularly sinister episode, opposition leaders were called in, supposedly for negotiations—then were promptly arrested when they arrived.

In January 2005, the Virgin's sanctuary was brazenly robbed in broad daylight. Hundreds of thousands of pesos, around three thousand U.S. dollars, and the Virgin's jewels—worth millions of pesos—were stolen. The parish priest was beaten, kidnapped, and left tied to a tree on a hillside outside of town until he was found several hours later. In private conversations, he shows the scars from his ordeal.

Indicative of the general climate of suspicion, a peculiar rumor circulated, that the pastor, himself implicated in the robbery, had himself arranged to be beaten and tied up so that he could not be accused of the theft. The priest was reassigned, but death threats continued, and later that year, Oaxaca's Human Rights Network issued a formal complaint asking that the incident be more assiduously investigated.

In the meantime, the political crisis deepened. On the last day of January, a leader of the Citizens' Movement was shot and killed in an altercation outside the municipal offices next to the church. His body lay sprawled and bleeding on the floor of the sanctuary atrium. In early February, stores on the main plaza were set afire. Later that month, another conflict caused a second death. Violence broke out again in March and April, on the latter occasion resulting in three dead, ten or twelve wounded, and more than seventy people arrested—after seven hours of confrontation with police in full riot gear on the plaza in front of the sanctuary.

To culminate this litany of disgrace, during Holy Week, the Virgin's crown was stolen.

Visitors to its sanctuary, however, seldom perceive the tension that inhabitants of Juquila suffer; they have come with a single purpose, to lay eyes on the Virgin.

*   *   *   *   *

A flat, round stained-glass image of the Virgin in white robes is set like a compass into the front façade of the sanctuary. The vast, broad atrium of the church, adjacent to the municipal offices, is gated. To the left-hand side of the church, pilgrims can enter a rectangular room heated with the suffocating warmth of rows and rows of candles whose fumes thicken my throat and make my eyes smart. A nondescript copy of the original virgin, perched among the flames of hundreds of candles, receives *milagritos* and photos (though not as avidly as the statue at the Pedimento). Sometimes fellow pilgrims do "cleansings" on each other, taking an unlit candle and passing it over the other person in a gesture of purification, then lighting it and leaving it for the Virgin.

In the area behind the church building, pilgrims can mingle, rest, or sleep. Two open dormitories (really three walls, a roof, and tiled floors), one for men and the other for women, provide places for pilgrims to lay sleeping mats or blankets. Oftentimes it is here that pilgrims from different places strike up conversations and exchange testimonies; in our case, having five fair-haired children—two of whom are twins—in tow was a definite conversation starter. Our most moving encounter took place with a young couple from a coastal village. They had come so that the husband could pass under the Virgin's veil before leaving on his first trip to the North.

A wide platform with a painted panorama is available for those who wish to have their photo taken against a facsimile of Juquila's bucolic scenery. There is a place for alcoholics to make sobriety vows and for chauffeurs to receive blessings. Holy water flows from a font at which pilgrims eagerly collect water (outside the atrium gates, children sell brightly colored plastic jugs, such as the ones you would use when you run out of gas, for this purpose). Periodically, blessed oil is brought out and poured into small clay pots to be taken home by pilgrims. Flowers, too, once they have adorned the sanctuary, are brought here to be given out: the Virgin's economy dictates that space be cleared for the next set of pilgrims' offerings through redistribution.

Steps lead from this area to the market below, where thousands of religious goods and tourist items are sold. At the head of the stairs, the parish runs its own gift shop. Even the poorest of pilgrims can take home a holy card with the Virgin's picture, sold for one *peso* (less than ten cents). I asked the salespeople if other *gringos* have come here, and they responded, "No." However, on second thought, they corrected themselves: occasionally a migrant returning from the North brings a white spouse.

Migration runs as a sub-text through the contemporary Juquila narrative, evidenced in many subtle forms, as understated and obvious as the indigenous identity of Santa Catarina Juquila. Returning migrants frequently visit Juquila to seek the Virgin's blessing or to offer thanks for favors received. Some have been displaced to other parts of Mexico; others have traveled further abroad, to distant areas in the United States. Vendors in Juquila sell miniature dollar bills as well as *pesos* for pilgrims to pin to the Virgin's cloak. The Virgin's feast day falls in December, the month during which many migrants who *can* return home *do*. Undocumented immigrants who cannot make the trip themselves commission relatives to make the pilgrimage. I once read about farm workers in Florida whose baby was born with birth defects; the child's grandparents made the trip from Michoacán to Juquila.

If Juquila represents the essence of indigenous, rural Mexico, pilgrimage in Latin America finds heightened symbolism in the steps of migrants. My friend the rural anthropologist has had to revise her basic demographic panorama: "There are now *three* Mexicos: the rural, the urban, and the Mexico in the United States."[20] During the years from 1995 to 2000, Mexican emigration rose to 350,000 people leaving home yearly. From 2000 to 2005, more than 550,000 Mexicans crossed the border each year. In 2006, emigration peaked at 580,000 and then dipped to level off in a plateau. Mexico is the foremost migrant-sending country in the world.[21]

Migrants from sending communities today have precedents in the *campesinos* among them who made the journey north half a century ago as contracted farm workers. However, in a new migratory pattern, since 1995 (when the dismantling of the countryside was felt in earnest), Mexican migrants have arrived not only to the areas in the United States that have historically received them, but to new areas as well, such as rural Georgia or upstate New York. On the road to Juquila, we saw vehicles bearing license plates from Illinois, California, North Carolina, Washington, Oregon, and Texas. Overwhelming numbers of migrants come from Mexican states foremost in sending pilgrims to Juquila. Oaxaca, Puebla, Veracruz, and Guerrero are now included in the country's top ten migrant-sending states. Their emigrants—modern-day pioneers—have literally opened new trails of travel and connection between the North and South.

But the migrant journey, like pilgrimage to Juquila, is fraught with hazard. The same year that the Free Trade Agreement took effect, increased vigilance caused migrants to venture into dangerous, isolated desert areas. Since Operation Gatekeeper was put into place, between 350 and 500 migrants (Mexicans and non-Mexicans) have died each year on the U.S.–Mexico border. At the time of this writing, since 1994, at least 5,600 people have lost their lives in the attempt to cross over.[22]

The risk of danger does not abate completely once migrants cross the border—it simply changes form. Undocumented migrants and immigrants, especially, perform the most dangerous and most poorly compensated jobs in our national economy. They reside in the worst living conditions and have the least access to health care. During our years in New York, my husband and I were shocked by the number of dead bodies our immigrant community sent home.

The perils migrants face are not only physical and socio-political but also spiritual and psychological. The human condition makes all people susceptible to sin. Evil exists within communities as well as outside them; temptation lurks within persons, as well as around them. Depression, addiction, and illness—as well as tragedies, accidents, and deportations—form part of immigrant communities' lives.

As in the case of the Virgin of San Juan de los Lagos in Jalisco, who became a patroness of migrants because *her people* became migrants, the Virgin of Juquila—already associated with travel—extends her protection over both sides of the border.

If anyone needs protection, it is migrants. The Juquilita's intercession spreads over them like a mantle, much as it once covered the citizens of Constantinople to protect them from harm. The ancient Eastern Virgin of the Veil has been reincarnated in Santa Catarina Juquila as
the Madonna of Migrants. The Juquilita's veil looks like a *mantilla* but
functions as a mother's *rebozo*, covering her children in their everyday
trials and tribulations. She gathers to herself especially those who have
journeyed and have now come "home" to a village that looks like their
village, to rest in her safe embrace.

This is it—the climax, the end of our long journey—and these are
its last steps: across the atrium, up the half-flight of stone stairs leading past a room with candles burning, around the circular ambulatory
to another half-flight of steps. The culminating moment of this pilgrimage is to stand in stillness—utter, complete, *non*-movement—
with lips quieted and heart racing, tears streaming, under the Virgin's
mantle. All those perilous, nerve-racking miles end in one holy, perfect moment in this refuge, this thin place. Hours of sweating under
the scorching hot sun or shivering under the brilliant stars, just to
have her veil brush against the top of my head, to kiss the dusty lace,
to run fingers over the outspread white mantle, to climb those final
stairs, and, at last . . . to arrive.

* * * * *

The Zapotecs we met from Guelatao pick tobacco in the fields of North
Carolina. The hotel owner's husband sends money from Manhattan;
our Chatino busboy worked for two years in a Chinese restaurant in
Virginia. When I asked the delegation from Puebla about their hometown, they disclosed that half their village works in New York. Our university friend speaks often of her sister, living now in the Los Angeles
area. Another of our student neighbors, a Chatino Juquileño, speaks
fluent English: he spent five years in Minnesota. The Nahua family we
talked to at the Pedimento follows the crops in California to save up for
the two-story house whose model they fashioned out of clay. (The
younger members of the family demanded to know why our immigration
policies discriminated against them; we could find no satisfactory reply.)

Returning migrants at Juquila inspired the insight that "un-
locked" for me the Juquila experience. From devout Catholics who
left their home villages for cities in Mexico or for a destination in the

North, I have heard a repeated concern. In trading a rural for an urban setting, or one's own homeland for a foreign country, emigrants face difficult experiences and culturally different religious practices which can, at times, prove alienating. There are more material distractions in the prosperous North, while simultaneously, the collective spiritual life is poorer. Keeping spiritually centered—a challenge for believers of any religion or background—becomes an extraordinary feat.

It is difficult to keep one's gaze fixed, to arrive to the end of the migrant journey—however it ends. Will it end in a raised ranch with a thirty-year mortgage in a U.S. suburb? In premature death in an accident or on the job? Or—the ideal—back in one's home village, in a concrete two-story house with truck in the yard, surrounded by grandchildren who listen to tales of adventures in *el Norte*?

It is difficult to keep one's gaze fixed when the body is put through trial after trial, not only in illegally crossing a border but also through years of manual labor (most immigrant men I know work two or three shifts, at jobs too heavy, too dirty, or too tedious for non-immigrants' tastes). It is hard to maintain one's composure during the hardest times of being away, such as the December *fiestas* and and the patronal feast of one's village or town, or when important events take place back home. As the years pass and emigration bleeds the countryside, it is hard not to succumb to depression as one's sending village empties. Only memories are left—of the fathers and mothers, aunts and uncles, nieces and nephews, sons and daughters, *compadres* and neighbors who have gone away. Memories and the reality of the rains that don't come as they should. And the land, the stubborn, enduring promise of the land.

Streamers adorn the threshold
of the sanctuary in Juquila

The beloved Virgin beckons from her pedestal. At her widest, she measures only about four inches; she stands just a foot tall. Her small nut-brown face barely visible, hair flowing over opulent robes, she shines like a morning star high above the altar. The statue is adorned with doll-sized jewels given by devotees. The preferred colors for her gowns are white and pastel pink, colors suited to a young girl. It is said that so many vestments have been donated to the sanctuary that the wearing of each dress (with which she will be clothed for only one day) has to be scheduled ten years in advance.

The exquisite appearance of the delicate statue promises a triumph of spiritual beauty over an unkind, ugly reality. True to the Immaculate Conception motif on which she is styled, the Juquilita reveals the Mother of God as untainted by sin or corruption. The human Mary of Nazareth went before us, body and soul, into heaven; she prefigures the glorious transformation that awaits her Son's followers. The dainty Virgin of Juquila—whimsical as a child, and as generous—symbolizes the primacy of God's little ones. Chosen by God the Father before the dawn of time, she is elevated by believers as the sign of an eschatological promise. No matter what their sins, or problems, or the tragedies they suffer, devotees believe that purification *can* happen; grace *can* be regained.

Pilgrims discover at Juquila an authentic expression of their contemporary spiritual journey. Like the first virgin (the ancient dark grandmother of the Pedimento), our outward lives look worn, battered, and scarred, as if bluntly hewn from rough wood. But our inward lives—our lives of *faith*—shine like this glittering, jeweled statue: precious, virginal, pure, and new.

Compared to the height of the niche above the altar, the place of the congregation is low in the sanctuary, and devotees take an even lower position by kneeling. In fact, in completing the long journey, many pilgrims cross the threshold of the church on their knees. Gazes fixed on the Virgin's image, candles and flowers in hand, they mouth prayers as they slowly, painfully inch toward the guardrail.

If pilgrimage takes on heightened symbolism because of migration, then this is its perfect expression. The act of a pilgrim approaching the altar on his or her knees, eyes fixed ardently on the image, is an enactment of the interior journey. It is not that political organizing and legislative change such as domestic policies to stem the flow of emigration are not important. It is that Juquila keeps alive the conviction that propels movement *toward* those actions, coming from that invisible, causative realm that addresses underlying existential questions. Pilgrimage to Juquila reveals that the Virgin's children may become displaced, but they can never be lost, because they are under her mantle.

Placing themselves under the Virgin's powerful patronage, believers kneel in an awareness of their own fragility and humility in God's divine presence. This posture is symbolically a sign of submission as well as repentance. But the kneeling pilgrims' eyes are fixed unwaveringly on the image that, for centuries, has traveled with them and for them. Known to secure divine mercy for her children in the past, she intercedes because she understands their needs. She is also small. She has also suffered. She has chosen voluntarily to accompany her children on their journeys, no matter where these may take them, no matter what the cost.

The people of God in massive migration testifies at Juquila, *We have survived to come this far.* Life's adversities bring us to our knees. Yet, we are not conquered. Seemingly an act of surrender, this posture carries an undercurrent of resistance. Utterly humble and devout, it is, at the same time, defiant, as if saying, *I may be on my knees—but nobody controls my gaze.*

The Virgin stands as witness to the simplest testimonies of faith. No matter how desperate the petition, she hears it. No matter how humble the offering made, she accepts it. Her motherhood is constant and authentic in a world of change and movement. Covering her children with her protective veil, she embraces them with unconditional love. Pilgrims' eyes may be fixed on her face, but their gaze does not stop there. Their gaze is fixed on eternity. And her face is the window, the portal, the door through which they get there.

III

Desde el cielo una hermosa
  mañana
La Guadaupana bajó al Tepeyac.

One lovely morning from heaven
To Tepeyac descended the Virgin.

Suplicante juntaba sus manos
Y eran mexicanos su porte y su faz.

Her supplicant hands and her face
Were the color of our race.

Su llegada llenó de alegría
De luz y armonía a todo el
  Anahuac.

Her arrival filled the whole valley
With light, joy and harmony.

Junto al monte pasaba Juan Diego
Y acercóse luego al oír cantar.

Juan Diego, walking along,
Approached on hearing the birds'
  song.

Juan Diegüito, la Virgen le dijo
Este cerro elijo para ser mi altar.

Dear Juan Diego, on this hill,
  said she
An altar must be built for me.

En su tilma entre rosas pintada
Su imagen amada se dignó dejar.

On his cloak, painted among roses
Her beloved image she left for us.

Desde entonces para el mexicano
Ser guadalupano es algo esencial.

Since then, to be Guadalupan
Is essential to being Mexican.

En sus penas se postra de hinojos
Y eleva sus ojos hacia el Tepeyac.

On our knees, when problems
  arise,
Toward Tepeyac we turn our eyes.

*Runners carry the image of the Virgin of Guadalupe
into a church in Newburgh, New York*

THE MOTHER'S GAZE

* * * * * * * * * * *

With the Revelation of the Second Person of the Trinity, the ability to image God comes through the physical presence of Jesus, and that is thanks to Mary.
— Constantine Cavarnos

After a prayer session at a migrant camp in New York's apple country, a young mother pauses on the steps of the crowded trailer she and her husband share with three other couples. When she feels overwhelmed by her life as an undocumented migrant far from home, she confides, she comes out onto these rickety steps to look for the Virgin's star in the night sky. Her grandmother taught her this custom in their Zapotec village in Oaxaca. "It helps me to know that whether I am here or in Mexico, I can see her," she says. After a moment, she adds in a quiet yet firm voice, "She sees me, too."

My hometown and its surrounding farmlands in New York State make an unlikely setting for the apparition of an indigenous Latin American Madonna. Yet, experiences like these have made me, too, glimpse her presence.

Perhaps it's not completely incongruous that while my Guadalupan fervor was awakened two decades ago south of the border, it flourished in a topography quite different from the terrain of Mexico. Crossing borders has long been integral to Marian tradition; after all, at the end of her lifetime, the Virgin herself was taken across the ultimate threshold into heaven, body and soul.

Since its inception, devotion to the Virgin of Guadalupe has shown remarkable flexibility and vigor in traversing boundaries. The celebrated patroness of a famous Marian sanctuary in Extremadura had crossed the ocean with conquering Spanish soldiers. Once the Mexican Virgin of

81

Guadalupe made her appearance, missionaries set out from colonial Mexico carrying likenesses of *la Guadalupana*, recognizable for her trademark iconography, to other parts of the Americas, such as Ponce, Puerto Rico, and as far away as the Philippines. Sharing her name with the Spanish counterpart who preceded her, the Mexican Guadalupe became established in the New World as a distinctly *American* virgin in a continent whose internal boundaries were not yet fixed.

The Guadalupan image is famously common in Texas and the Southwest, where generations of Mexican-Americans preceded later-arriving Anglo settlers (Mexican-Americans from U.S. states that formerly belonged to Mexico preserve this historical memory in the saying, "We didn't cross the border, *it* crossed *us*").

But as Mexican migrants and immigrants have made their way into new areas of the North that were unacquainted with Mexican immigration until relatively recently—places like the tobacco fields of Kentucky, the meat-packing plants of Milwaukee, or the factories and farms of New York—migrant and immigrant communities have had to introduce the devotion themselves in unfamiliar settings, to varying degrees of resistance.

In Oaxaca, I experienced in reverse the nostalgia of the immigrant community I had left. During the three years we lived in Mexico, I always felt most homesick on December 12, the Virgin's feast day! The typical elements of our Guadalupan celebrations in New York, I came to realize, had acquired a heightened devotional pitch in the North. The singing of traditional hymns, all the more bittersweet for not being heard for the rest of the year; the *Antorcha*, a lit torch run by foot in arduous pilgrimage all the way from Mexico City; the dizzying aroma of thousands of roses procured in the dead of winter; and most of all, the masses of adherents—who achieve a tremendous collective presence when gathered at the same time in one place—come together with urgent poignancy as immigrant communities pay homage to the Virgin of Guadalupe.

Modern sensibility does not take easily to the idea of living, loving, *looking* icons. Yet, this is precisely the genius of the devotion centered on the Virgin of Guadalupe's image. Much like the icons used for veneration in the Eastern church, popular traditions of Our Lady of Guadalupe stem from a belief system in which her representations come to life. The tremendously rich and complex symbolism of Our Lady of Guadalupe, coupled with her remarkable agility in crossing borders, provides the matrix for an intimate relationship in which her eyes fasten on the beloved image of the other. In this interaction, the true identity of the object of her gaze comes to light. The Mother of God, because she knows her children, *sees* them.

The Virgin of Guadalupe holds adherents' attention not only because, as patroness of Mexico, she provides a unifying national symbol, and not only because, as Empress of the Americas, she reigns on a continent rapidly being globalized. She does both of these, but first and foremost she is a mother. The Virgin of Guadalupe's authentic identity is that of a loving mother who nurtures her children in a mutual, empowering relationship. And the way she accomplishes this is through her gaze.

*   *   *   *   *

The foundational narrative of the Guadalupan story is based on a legendary series of encounters between an indigenous convert, St. Juan Diego Cuauhtlatoatzin, and the Virgin Mary, recently arrived in the Americas at the time of the Conquest. Popularly referred to as *Las Apariciones*, "the Apparitions," these encounters are thoroughly embedded in the fabric of Mexican imagination and transmitted through popular practices. One well-circulated song, known commonly as *La Guadalupana* for its repetitive refrain, provides an accessible version of the story, a version my own children had memorized before they were old enough to understand its words.

During the colonial period, mention of the Guadalupan devotion was recorded in several literary works. The *Nican Mopohua* "Here it is written" is today considered by most devotees to be the most valuable of these early accounts. This document, thought to have been written in Nahuatl, outlines the stages of a developing relationship between Juan Diego Cuauhtlatoatzin and the Mother of God—a relationship that would ripple outward in ever-extending circles, in the Virgin's words, to "all those who inhabit this land, and to others who love me, as well."

The *Nican Mopohua* concurs with other documents of the colonial period in its presentation of the principal characters and basic plot of the Guadalupan event; it is unique, however, in its elaborate and evocative narration, which is told quite simply but with deep symbolism. Theologian Virgilio Elizondo has plumbed the *Nican Mopohua* with insight gained through years of study augmented by decades of pastoral experience in Mexican-American communities, resulting in a richly layered interpretation.[1]

Juan Diego, walking over the hill of Tepeyac on his way to hear Mass at a mission center in Tlatelolco, is intercepted by the Virgin Mary, who asks him to relay a message to the bishop. In the *Nican Mopohua*, the Virgin proclaims, "I ardently wish and greatly desire that a church be built for me here, where I will reveal...and give to people all my love, my compassion, my aid, and my protection, for it is I who am your compassionate mother...there I will hear their weeping and their sorrows in order to remedy and heal all their various afflictions, their miseries, and their torments."

Juan Diego accepts the Virgin's missive and, changing his route, delivers the message to an incredulous bishop (the *Nican Mopohua* names Franciscan Fray Juan de Zumárraga). Reporting back to the Virgin at the same site, Juan Diego asks that another delegate be selected—someone more credible in the eyes of Spanish ecclesial authorities. The colorful dialogue makes clear both that Juan Diego understands his inferior role in relation to the bishop *and* that the Virgin has chosen none other than him for this position as her emissary. Juan Diego returns to the bishop's palace and presents his case once again. This time, intrigued by his insistence, the bishop asks for "a sign" from the mysterious woman in order to corroborate the Indian's story. Zumárraga's servants follow Juan Diego in a futile attempt to foil his credibility, but lose sight of him. At Tepeyac, the Virgin assures Juan Diego that the next morning she will give him the proof he needs to satisfy the bishop.

Arriving at his home, however, Juan Diego finds his uncle deathly ill, and for the second time in the story sets out before dawn for Tlatelolco—this time, however, using an alternate route. In spite of his attempt to avoid her, the Virgin intercepts his path, and during this dialogue she assures him that his uncle has already been cured. Then she utters the words that form the climax of the dialogue, "Am I not here, who am your mother?" The pressing concern for his uncle's health resolved, Juan Diego follows the Virgin's order to bring back roses found on the summit of Tepeyac. He gathers them into his *tilma*, or cloak, and the Virgin touches them with her own hands before sending him yet again to Zumárraga's palace.

Though the servants—who perceive the fragrant aroma emanating through its rough fabric—try three times to wrest the garment from its owner, Juan Diego manages to obey the Virgin's directive that he allow no one to view the cloak's contents until he is standing in the presence of the bishop. Finally admitted to Zumárraga's presence, the Virgin's emissary opens his *tilma*, revealing not only roses but the image the Mother of God has sent as proof of her appearance.

The *tilma* (preserved in the Basilica of St. Mary of Guadalupe in Mexico City) plays an integral part of the Guadalupan devotion. Legend tells that the image of Our Lady of Guadalupe, unveiled in the presence of the Franciscan,[2] reproduces the Virgin as seen by Juan Diego Cuauhtlatoatzin during their encounters and by his uncle, Juan Bernardino, at the time of his miraculous healing.

The primary text of the apparition is, simply, the Virgin's presence, made concrete by the *tilma* and made literal by the proliferation of images that reproduce it.

As in the case of any apparition, the factuality of the encounters of two Nahuatl-speaking converts with the Virgin Mary cannot be scientifically proven or disproved. Even historical reconstruction, while illuminating the origins of a tradition, cannot confirm or discount a devotion's validity, since its ultimate authenticity rests not on material evidence but rather on the immeasurable religious experience of its adherents.

Yet, it must be admitted that the enigmatic origins of the *tilma* lend themselves to proponents' claims of its divine character. Many alterations have been worked upon the image over time, with new technologies allowing discoveries about its material composition, but the original underlying layer of the painting remains a mystery.

Scientific studies carried out toward the end of the last century corroborate what pious proponents of the devotion claimed during the colonial period: that, given the marsh environment of Tepeyac, the threads of the fabric, woven from plant fibers, should have disintegrated long ago. (One historical source notes that in the seventeenth century, devotees overlaid portions of the image with silver detail, only to see the silver disintegrate in the humidity.)

The pigments used in the undermost layer of the image still go unrecognized as paints from the palettes of either European or indigenous artists.[3] And, unlike the case of traditional European religious art, which made use of brushes to apply paint and which employed sketching as a first step in executing tapestries or other large works, infra-red imaging has not found evidence of brush-strokes or the tracing of a preliminary drawing before paints were applied.[4]

Then there is the enigma of the Virgin's gently half-closed eyes.

She stands with hands folded in prayer, her gaze fixed slightly beneath her and to her right, as if taking a scene into view. Her expression appears benign, with the fixedness of her gaze softened by the slight lowering of her eyelids (a more direct gaze would have looked harsh). Her angled body orients her countenance toward the viewer, her pose ingeniously integrating the seam of the cloak into the composition. When taking in the totality of the image, the viewer's gaze grazes the magnificent *mandorla* or body halo (a typically European motif), then shifts to the tunic—lingering on the detail work of the robe—before finally focusing in on her face, the folded hands in view. The result is an inviting visual connection, as if where once Juan Diego Cuauhtlatoatzin stood, the viewer now stands in his place at her feet.

If the familiar iconography (e.g., the sunburst around her figure, the moon under her feet) makes it easy for devotees to *see* her, the other half of the symbolic message is that the image triggers the experience of *being seen*.

The *tilma* preserves a distinctly intimate or personal character, as if the Virgin were still carrying on a one-on-one conversation with the recipient of her gaze; yet, the image's destiny as a collective ecclesial symbol is encoded in the story by the setting of the bishop's palace in which it was revealed. Although the narrative does not specify all the people who in later centuries were thought to have been present, various other characters mentioned in the story, including indigenous converts receiving catechesis, are inferred to have been in the room at the moment the painting was first seen.

In 1929 and again in 1951, Guadalupan experts, fascinated by the Virgin's enigmatic eyes, suggested that human figures could actually be seen reflected in them. Photographs of the Virgin's pupils were magnified and the prints studied for evidence. This element of Guadalupan popular tradition has been picked up and even embellished by the use of modern technology in recent years, making quite literal the suggestion that the Virgin sees her children: at the time of this writing, no fewer than thirteen human figures have been sighted in the Virgin's eyes![5]

In 1999, a scientist who has also studied the Shroud of Turin confirmed the evidence of three layers of redaction in the image. The first layer remains intriguingly indecipherable.[6] Additions or alterations appear to have been made before Our Lady of Guadalupe's rise in popularity as *La Criolla* (patroness of citizens of Spanish descent born in New Spain). These redactions make apparent a fluid process during which the content of the miraculous image was reinforced by integrating elements of intensely meaningful signs drawn from two different—and opposing—symbolic systems. The black sash around the Virgin's waist, which in Nahua imagery signifies pregnancy, and the hands with shortened fingers uphold her identification with the indigenous people. The angel or *putto*, which may have replaced bird wings at her feet, incorporates a typically European motif, as do the pose itself, the vine-and-leaf pattern on the Virgin's gown, and the crown which is thought to have at one time adorned her head (removed as *criollos* began to chafe under the Spanish Crown).

European religious art is known to have served as a means of catechetical instruction, especially for the non-literate believers who formed the majority of the Christian population. The Council of Trent defined norms for religious art, and the basic composition of the Guadalupan image follows motifs for representing the Immaculate Conception. For a sign to be credible, it had to be not only authentic but also orthodox, derived from identifiably Christian—not pagan—origin. (Spanish missionaries did not question the *existence* of indigenous deities, whom they saw as manifestations of the devil; their conquest consisted in overcoming them.) The *tilma*'s iconography fulfills this requisite.

At the same time, the use of a visual image for revelation coincides with the indigenous medium of codices used for recording important religious and historical events. Many interpretations of the image—for example, those found in the official website of the basilica in Mexico City—refer to the *tilma* as a codex, explicitly placing the image in the line of indigenous recorded tradition.

For the Spanish church (recently emerged from the Reconquista and still engaged in the Inquisition), the crescent moon represented Islam, and when the Virgin triumphantly strides the silver sliver under her feet, victory over "paganism" or heresy was implied. The inclusions of the sun, moon, and stars was a common feature of Immaculate Conception iconography, echoing the apocalyptic text in

Revelation 12 where a woman "clothed with the sun, with the moon under her feet, and on her head a crown of twelve stars" flees to find a safe place to give birth while a cosmic battle rages around her. Depictions of the Virgin Mary as the Immaculate Conception from different parts of Europe show the same iconographic pattern. However, as the official patroness of Spain and a favorite representation of Mary among conquistadors, the Immaculate Conception resonated particularly with the Spanish church's sense of being "chosen" both to save European Catholicism and to evangelize the New World.

The imposition of imagery from the dominating religion of an invading culture—which, make no mistake, fully intended to stamp out every vestige of idolatry—is hardly surprising; what is fascinating is the way in which the same motif coincides here with deeply rooted symbols of an indigenous religious worldview. The astronomical genius of the cultures of the area now known as Mexico and Central America had given rise to complex ritual calendars determined by the constellations. In the Aztec Empire, the view of the cosmos at the time of the Conquest (dictated through domination by the Mexica, a bellicose nomadic nation that had migrated from what is now Oklahoma to Central Mexico) held at its center Huitzilopochtli, the sun god, ruler of the Fifth Era.[7]

Some contemporary *guadalupanos* locate in the forty-six stars that adorn the Virgin's cloak all the constellations visible in the night sky of Anahuac. The apparition is dated during the winter solstice of 1531, a period that saw the culmination of a series of astronomical signs including Halley's comet and a solar eclipse.

Juan Diego's first Christian name recalls the attribution of the Fourth Gospel and of the Book of Revelation to the Beloved Disciple, John. His second name, also that of an apostle, honors the immensely popular Spanish Santiago (in colonial times, indigenous people were allowed to use only "Diego," the humbler form of the name "Santiago").

Juan Diego's original name, Cuauhtlatoatzin, is Nahuatl for "the eagle who sings [or speaks]." His home village, Cuautitlán, means "place of the eagle." The association with the eagle coincides with the iconographic representation of the evangelist John, the bird that, according to legend, accompanied him in the island of Patmos. (It is there that he is supposed to have written the Book of Revelation.) In Nahua symbolism, the eagle is emblematic of the Aztec Empire's own myth of origin. The nomadic Mexica were to wander in the desert until they saw the sign given to them by Huitzilopochtli: an eagle eating a serpent, perched atop a cactus.

The *tilma*, then, demonstrates a mastery of crossover between two symbol systems. Its earliest layer remains inviolate in its mystery, while subsequent adaptations provide a record of exchange between Christian and traditional native religions. Virgilio Elizondo identifies this crossover, encoded in the Guadalupan image itself, as the inauguration of *mestizaje* in the Americas—the mixing of European and indigenous sources that would come to characterize New Spain.[8] In her very person, Our Lady of Guadalupe brings about something new. While integrating the past, she orients devotees' gaze toward the apocalyptic vision poetically described by the writer of Revelation.

In doctrine, apparitions technically belong to the realm of personal revelation and therefore are not binding as dogma in the way that the Immaculate Conception or the Assumption, for example, constitute articles of belief. Yet devotion to the Virgin of Guadalupe—in tradition, with its origin rooted in the apparitions—has been given ecclesial sanction in an escalation of papal honors culminating in the canonization of Juan Diego Cuauhtlatoatzin in 2002. In 1737, Our Lady of Guadalupe was made patroness of Mexico City, and in 1754, of all of New Spain. In 1895, a coronation ceremony was held to formally recognize her sovereignty, and in 1910 she was declared Patroness of all Latin American countries (a patronage extended to the Philippines in 1935). In 1945, she was made Empress of the Americas.

Almost five centuries since the time of Juan Diego, Our Lady of Guadalupe continues to "appear"—on t-shirts, long-distance telephone cards, blankets, clocks, windshields, calendars, home altars, murals, and even the tattooed flesh of devotees. In one clever appropriation, a miniscule picture of the Virgin is encased in a clear plastic bead, tiny as a drop of dew, a picture that is visible when held up close to one squinting eye. As if to reinforce the devotion's foundational narrative, innumerable facsimiles of Our Lady of Guadalupe's image can be sighted throughout the Americas.

In the apparition story, Juan Diego was not the only believer to be seen by the Virgin; her message, after all, communicates concern for all her children in New Spain. The sorrows of the colonial-era populations of the Americas had come to her attention, in a continent whose borders were not yet formed. Like other native Christian converts, Juan Diego learned about the Mother of God from missionaries and was surely instructed that all Christians live under her watchful gaze. He was, however, among the first to see *her*.

✳ ✳ ✳ ✳ ✳

An economically depressed small city on the banks of the Hudson River, Newburgh was once a thriving factory town in a valley known for its fertile farmlands and abundant fishing. Now, Newburgh earns periodic distinctions of a more sobering variety (e.g., second place for homicides in the state of New York, one of the poorest cities of its size in the United States). Nearby farmlands are rapidly being converted into urban sprawl while urban decay erodes the life of its inner city.

Newburgh has always drawn newcomers seeking a better life; episodes of immigration define its basic history. Its original indigenous inhabitants having been displaced, successive waves of German, English, Irish, Polish, Italian, African-American, and Puerto Rican settlers landed on its riverbanks. At the turn of the past century, Newburgh already bore the reputation of a "typhoid town" for the poor living conditions in its neighborhoods, peopled by influxes of foreign and U.S.–born migrant workers.

Chapters of progress were written here, as well, their importance extending beyond Newburgh's limits. George and Martha Washington wintered here during the Revolutionary War. Thomas Alva Edison invented here. Newburgh residents took part in innovative experiments such as the telephone and the launching of the first steam ship. The city's strategic location as a port settlement and a railway stop enabled commerce to thrive here. The fertile farming towns in the area once depended on Newburgh for marketing their bounty, and its main street, "Broadway," was dug wide enough for herds to be driven down its long slope to the riverfront.

In recent decades, however, flight to suburban areas has left the city center bereft and abandoned. Like so many others, my own family moved out of Newburgh once the opportunity presented itself. The exodus from the inner city left numerous openings in rental housing and low-paying service and manufacturing jobs. True to Newburgh's historical pattern, the vacuum was filled by immigrants, now predominantly from Latin America. More than fifty years ago, New-burgh's then-thriving manufacturing industry attracted the first Puerto Rican workers to its factories; some forty years ago, small contingents of Argentinean, Honduran, and Peruvian immigrants established themselves in the area, joined soon afterward by Newburgh's first Mexican families.

The four Catholic parishes in Newburgh were founded respectively by waves of German, Polish, Italian, and Irish newcomers to this area. Nowadays, our parish attracts Spanish-speaking Catholics from all over the Hudson Valley, celebrating special feast days for Argentineans, Colombians, Cubans, Dominicans, Ecuadorians, Hondurans, Mexicans, Peruvians, Puerto Ricans, and Salvadorans.

Most community organizers in Newburgh consider census figures for Latinos to be underrepresentative. The number of undocumented immigrants who slip from view is difficult to gauge, and the Spanish-speaking population is growing so quickly that numbers soon become outdated. Statistics gathered in the 2000 census calculated the Latino population as comprising over a third of the city's inhabitants; a population update starting only five years later increased the estimate to almost half. Furthermore, while not living within its limits, immigrants who live in smaller communities throughout the area come to the city to frequent its stores and services. During the Guadalupan celebrations, Spanish-speaking immigrants from the entire area (not exclusively Mexican) converge to render honor to their common mother.

I grew up in Newburgh without ever seeing (much less *eating*) a tortilla. Now, two tortilla companies based in Newburgh package their product for distribution throughout the United States.

The pattern of growth of Mexican and Mexican-American presence in my hometown is best illustrated by the development of the celebration of the Virgin of Guadalupe's feast day. The December twelfth observance started in a basement in the very neighborhood where I had grown up. One of the founding families of the Mexican community—still quite small at that time—began to host a yearly prayer service and meal. Convening extended family members and others from their village, they sang Guadalupan hymns and recited the rosary in the presence of an image that reproduces the painting on Juan Diego's *tilma*. The hosting family would organize a huge feast to follow the religious ceremony, with dishes prepared from ingredients procured through great effort (at that time, Mexican products were still hard to find).

When the number of participants grew too large for the celebration to be held in a house, the feast moved to a Catholic parish with Spanish-speaking services (pioneered by the city's sizeable Puerto Rican population). With the support of the parish and of the members of the diverse Hispanic countries of origin in the congregation, a huge reproduction of the Virgin of Guadalupe was brought up from the basilica. The celebration continued as a small but steadily growing event in Newburgh—until the thousands of Mexican emigrants from rural Puebla began to arrive.

While Newburgh's Latino population is diverse, made up of residents from multiple countries of origin, Mexican emigration made its numbers explode. As Mexico's economic policies were rewritten for the North American Free Trade Agreement, an exodus journey began. Beginning in 1993, a wave of displaced small farmers and their families from all over the Republic set out for *el otro lado*, the other side of the border. So many emigrants from the state of Puebla came to New York that a new name was coined: *Pueblayork*.

Many villages that send emigrants to the Mid-Hudson River Valley are located along *la Ruta Dominicana*, the route that Dominican mis-

Little boy from Newburgh, New York, dressed as St. Juan Diego

sionaries established from Puebla to Oaxaca in the Mixteca region. Most are settlements made up of the descendants of former *hacienda* workers who gained farmlands after Mexico's Revolution only to lose them to the Free Trade Agreement. While the sending area extends from Izúcar de Matamoros all the way to Acatlán de Osorio, the communities clustered around Tehuitzingo, in particular, have close connections with Newburgh, their emigrants' principal destination. In Puebla, schoolteacher Juan Perez estimates that some 40 percent of the population of the area around

Tehuitzingo has been leached by emigration. In some communities, however, the rate may be even higher. In the hometown of the family that hosted Newburgh's first Guadalupan celebration in a basement, 90 percent of the villagers have left in search of work, leaving 80 percent of its households vacant.

By 1995, Mexican and Central American farm workers in the Hudson River Valley outnumbered the Jamaican and Haitian fruit pickers who in recent decades had formed the majority of the area's seasonal agricultural laborers.

The already-established immigrant families from the sending region of the Mixteca, joined by other immigrants from various communities of origin, now began to orchestrate the December twelfth celebration on a much larger scale. Immigrants often work two or even three jobs, but organizers began to take on the time-consuming task of planning for the intensive participation that characterizes patronal feasts. Arrangements were made with the pastor for the *mañanitas*, an early morning chorus to be sung before dawn, a practice that grows each year. Lavish floral pieces are donated by the small business owners who suddenly benefit from the influx of new patrons. *Bailables*, folkloric dances, complete with costumes and props, are practiced for weeks before being performed during the festival that follows Mass. Until Newburgh residents formed their own mariachi ensemble, musicians were sought at great expense from larger communities in the boroughs of New York City or New Jersey. The celebratory meal (now served for several hundred people) entails the culinary talents of scores of women who compete to proffer the best *mole* in honor of the Virgin. The small celebration that had started off in a basement apartment and had existed in relative

Little girl from Middletown, New York, dressed as the Virgin of Guadalupe

anonymity in a historically Irish parish suddenly became the single largest religious celebration in the city, outside of Holy Week.

In other places in the Northeast where Mexican immigration is a relatively new phenomenon, establishing local December twelfth celebrations has not always been easy. Some communities, especially in rural and suburban areas, do not have pre-existing Hispanic congregations for newer Latinos to integrate into. Even the simplest of traditional gestures can become complicated where local churches have not yet developed pastoral ministry for a new wave of immigrants.

Finding a Spanish-speaking priest and a receptive parish can seem no more or less insurmountable than convincing a bishop of an apparition. Quite apart from language barriers, there are cultural differences between European-American and Latin American Catholic religious practices. These are made obvious, for example, when *guadalupanos* ask that the church be opened at 5 AM for the Virgin's early morning serenade.

These divisions become even more pronounced in the civil sphere—where as a socio-political group, immigrants of any ethnic background or national origin may meet indifference or even hostility. A notable example is the Guadalupan procession. In most places, a municipal permit must be obtained for devotees to carry an image through the streets. The *antorcha* (a relay run with a lit torch) heightens a procession's intensity. Explaining to a harried city clerk why traffic should be stopped for a torch to be run through the streets requires a great deal of cultural dexterity. And yet, like Juan Diego who had to return to the bishop's palace several times before being believed, obstacles to the celebration increase participants' investment in it. Much is at stake, for when the Virgin becomes visible, her children become visible as well.

In making *her* publicly seen, *guadalupanos* emerge from anonymity. One sociologist observes that in areas newly receiving Mexican immigrants, even if this demographic group's *numbers* are recognized (assuming the undocumented are accurately counted), their *presence* is not. Taking the Virgin of Guadalupe from the domestic sphere to the civil arena, especially the streets, means forcing a recognition of her existence—and, by extension, the right of her children to claim their place in the public eye.

For *guadalupanos*, however, the object of *their* gaze is the Virgin herself. In Newburgh, the main attraction of the yearly December twelfth celebration in our parish is the enormous framed reproduction of the *tilma* ensconced in the nave of the church.

Though devotees are exposed to many reproductions of Our Lady of Guadalupe on a daily basis—her image can be found in Latin American homes and businesses as well as in vehicles—something different happens when adherents *contemplate* her icon. For our Latino immigrant community in Newburgh, during those moments when devotees gather at her feet, her image seems to come alive. The recognition of her figure (which "travels" with ease due to her trademark features that even a child can identify) triggers a sense of comfort and familiarity. But *looking at* her picture with concentrated focus and undivided attention brings about a much deeper experience, as if the viewer actually stands before her.

The Virgin's gaze differs from the indiscriminate (and often discriminat*ing*) gaze of the dominant culture that overlooks particularities between Latinos who are lumped together as "Hispanics."⁹ Furthermore, the dominant culture often fails to regard undocumented immigrants as persons entitled to the most basic of human rights. The motherly gaze of Our Lady of Guadalupe takes in each devotee in his or her own context in all its fullness. Because she is their mother, she knows quite well who her children are and where they come from.

This experience is heightened by *communitas*, especially prayer in community. Latinos of other countries of origin join Mexican members of our parish and Spanish speakers who have come from other places for the December twelfth celebration. Invariably, my mind is flooded with memories of my grandmother . . . of my parents' house of hospitality . . . of the visits to Mexico that set the course for my adulthood. I am overcome with gratitude for the pilgrimage of my life, a journey that has brought me to *this* church at *this* moment, in a city I never expected to return to, at this particular time of Newburgh's growth.

Standing before the image in a church crammed with devotees, singing hymns that recount the apparition, a palpable shock of longing and recognition shudders through the crowd. The experience is definitely cathartic—a dose of familiarity for *guadalupanos* far from home and the release of emotion enabled by the practice of customs, for the most part, neglected the rest of the year. It is transformative as well, a communal mystical encounter in which Our Lady of Guadalupe's image brings devotees into her very presence. When they look at her image, it is as if the Virgin looks back. Under her gaze, a sense of peace and reassurance descends like a mantle cast over the gathered assembly; a people comes home.

* * * * *

St. John Damascene called religious images "precise means of remembering"; for *guadalupanos*, Our Lady of Guadalupe acts as a powerful catalyst for waking to a spiritual reality always present but rarely perceived. No matter where they are, devotees of the Virgin of Guadalupe can receive her "apparition." In this interaction, they are reminded of their true identities: the beloved children of a powerful, empowering mother. As in the case of the young mother who steps out of her trailer to gaze up at "the Virgin's star," even a brief moment of contemplation serves to center those who seek her.

The magnetism of the Basilica of St. Mary of Guadalupe, where the Virgin first appeared, draws some twenty million pilgrims a year, making it the most visited Christian shrine in the world. Departing or returning migrants of many Latin American countries of origin pay homage there. Merely approaching the walls of the sanctuary overwhelms visitors with emotion. However, Tepeyac—as the location where the Virgin meets her children in a transformative encounter—can be anywhere. Like the proverbial Zen circle whose center is everywhere and whose circumference is nowhere, wherever a devotee finds her image, the Virgin herself can be met.

In Newburgh, my husband and I hosted a migrant who was returning from a trip back to Mexico, this time with a nineteen-year old from Puebla on his first trip to the North. They soon found jobs at a nearby farm. As they prepared to leave, we gave them lapel pins of the Virgin of Guadalupe. The young friend had resisted any display of emotion during the long and difficult trip with other undocumented migrants crossing the border; he bore stoically the first days of immersion in a foreign setting and the shock of a New York winter. Now, at the sight of the miniature replica with its familiar icon, he averted his face to hide the quick tears that flowed spontaneously.

Another migrant, originally from Veracruz, carries in his wallet a holy card he received during Mass at a farm-worker camp several years ago. Its edges are tattered and its image has faded, but the trademark icon of the Virgin of Guadalupe is still recognizable. The Mass had coincided with his hitting bottom as an alcoholic, and his recovery—which, as anyone who is familiar with alcoholism can attest, really *is* miraculous—became intrinsically related to the Virgin whose image he contemplates whenever he feels like drinking. This *guadalupano* went on to found the first Spanish-speaking chapter of Alcoholics Anonymous in the nearby city of Poughkeepsie.

The *tilma* and the devotional practices that surround it concretize a simple supposition of popular religion—one that runs contrary to the contemporary Western view of religious art. Latin American popular understandings of sacred images have a great deal in common with the Eastern spirituality of icons. This spirituality conceptualizes icons as "windows" to the sacred realm, endowing them with a literal quality of direct access to the divine in an attitude toward images that is nowadays absent in mainstream Western societies.

The Orthodox spirituality of icons, reintroduced relatively recently to Roman Catholic believers, takes a distinctive approach to religious art. Unlike Western art, in which a material representation inspires or interprets a spiritual reality but remains a lifeless image, representations of Christ and the saints open human eyes to the divine presence, or in another metaphor, awaken our consciousness as one opens one's eyes upon waking from sleep. Icons operate actively, functioning in a way that is different from that of objects of Western religious art, which can instruct or edify but which do not often "awaken" viewers. Icon scholar Constantine Cavarnos wrote in his book, *Orthodox Iconography*:

> We have a tendency to forget, to forget even things that are of vital importance to us, to fall asleep spiritually. So even though we may *know* many things about the Christian faith, such as the commandment of love, the teaching about the spiritual realm, the exemplary character and noble deeds of many holy personages, we tend to *forget* them, as we become preoccupied with everyday worldly matters and pursuits. Icons serve to *remind* us of these things, to awaken us with respect to them.[10]

The radical thinker Ivan Illich articulates a fundamental difference between the philosophy of optics in antiquity and our contemporary understanding of vision. In the ancient world, visual perception was regarded as a mutual happening; the viewer was considered an active participant in the seeing process. Unlike a camera lens which needs only to be opened or shut in order to allow a visual imprint to *come in*, the viewer's gaze was thought to *go out* to meet the object of perception.

The philosophy of active sight necessary for contemplation of religious images was preserved in the East but—at least in dominant religious expression—lost in the West. Traditions in popular religion retained something of this approach to Christian sacred art, gaining vigor when grafted to native spiritualities in the lands where Christianity arrived. Based in the theology of the Incarnation, where Christ redeems not only human beings but the entire material world, the spirituality of icons allows believers to experience the divine presence through nature transformed by human piety and artistry.

In the treatment of icons in the Eastern Church—as in Latin American popular religious practice—once a completed image is blessed, it partakes of the life of the sacred person it portrays. A sense of the miraculous often surrounds the origin of images. Like the Eastern icons that are "windows" to the sacred, in Latin American popular traditions, religious images are a category in themselves—not merely decoration, but vehicles to a spiritual realm.

When this supposition is taken *too* literally, of course, statues or paintings actually betray Christ or the saint whom they represent. One of the great religious ironies of the Latin American panorama is that the central complaint of Catholic missionaries has rebounded over the centuries to be voiced on the lips of contemporary Protestant evangelicals: idolatry. The rise of fundamentalist Pentecostalism in recent decades sharply divides communities with regard to religious images, denounced as "idols."

Eastern Orthodox theology clarifies the position of the icon quite simply. St. Basil the Great (upheld in the eighth century by St. John Damascene) insisted that religious art links believers spiritually to the "prototype" of the personage being represented. The image is not an idol, that is, a material object receiving *latreia*, adoration proper to God. Reverence to an icon, *timetike proskynesis*, "passes over" to the saint or to Christ whom it portrays, and in turn, ultimately to the Godhead who is the Creator of all. Understood in this framework, the icon serves not only as a window, but as a border. A permeable boundary made to be crossed, the religious image delivers believers into the divine presence.

Debates about the authorship of the miraculous picture on St. Juan Diego's *tilma* date from the earliest years of Guadalupan tradition. In fact, the earliest historical record of the devotion comes in a rebuttal of its orthodoxy under the charge that idolatry of a pagan goddess was being perpetrated in the veneration of the image. Evidence cited was the fact that native Christians called the Virgin of Guadalupe *Tonantzin*, a collective possessive term for "Our Dear Mother." The rumor circulated that an indigenous painter named Marcos had composed the already famous—and already controversial—image. Refutations of this unfounded attribution are echoed today by contemporary historians.

Centuries removed from the Conquest, it is difficult for modern day readers to imagine the shock waves that reverberated through Europe upon the "discovery" of the Americas, a vast continent containing countless native nations that had been absent from the panorama of Christian geography. A first theological step—inconceivable to contemporary Christians, yet necessary for Europeans in order to reconfigure their worldview—was to debate whether indigenous people had souls. The resolution of this absurd hypothetical question carried extreme importance, for if native Americans did not have souls, they could be enslaved by Catholic invaders who would be legally entitled to consider them less than fully human.

The apparition story did more than simply provide a definitive answer to the sixteenth-century theological debates in Europe about whether indigenous people had souls. The devotion, centered on the miraculous image, opened new avenues for understanding the Incarnation in the Americas. Within the womb of Mary of Nazareth, the invisible Godhead took on human flesh and became visible; in the Americas, the apparition of the Virgin of Guadalupe made Christ present yet again, and the *tilma* provided concrete "proof" of the divine Incarnation.

The Virgin Mary, in scripture named as the mother of Jesus and in Catholic tradition made mother of all Christians by Christ on the cross, is in essence a maternal symbol, but in the *tilma* and the images that reproduce it, Our Lady of Guadalupe's motherhood is communicated through the use of indigenous symbolism.

The Virgin, in popular parlance affectionately called *La Morenita* for her dark skin, shares the warm color of her indigenous and *mestizo* children. A prayer printed on mass-produced candles such as the kind sold in supermarkets or *botánicas* states bluntly, "By choosing to take on our color, you joined yourself to our race."

Her pregnancy, introduced into the iconography unmistakably through the black sash, integrates a custom foreign to European art into the painting. The Spanish Guadalupe housed in Estremadura (birthplace of many notorious conquistadors) is a Black Madonna, a statue of mother and child hewn from dark wood. And an image in the choir loft of the Spanish sanctuary modeled on the Immaculate Conception bears such a likeness to the Mexican painting that one historian suggests that the similarity may have caused the colonizers to settle on "Guadalupe" as the identity of the American-born virgin[11] whom Nahuatl speakers first called *Coatlalupeuh,* "She Who Crushes the Head of the Serpent." The rare visual portrayal of a *pregnant* virgin, however, introduces the innovation of an indigenous garment that implies that its wearer is with child.

The Virgin's maternity is rendered through indigenous terms in the oral narrative as well. In the *Nican Mopohua,* Our Lady of Guadalupe's motherhood—defined through her relationship to her indigenous children—comes to the fore. From the very first dialogue, a sense of kinship is established as the mysterious woman speaks to Juan Diego in Nahuatl, calling him by name and addressing him as her son.

Juan Diego meets the Mother of God on the hill of Tepeyac. According to Franciscan missionary and ethnographer Bernardino de Sahagún, this was a pilgrimage site formerly dedicated to Tonantzin, identified in some traditions as a virgin mother. The patroness of herbs, associated with healing (a detail that intersects with the cure of Juan Diego's uncle), this deity preferred animal to human sacrifice, which scholars believe had spiraled to staggering numbers as Mexica rulers attempted to maintain their dominion over other indigenous nations in the Aztec Empire.

In the text, the Mother of God does not call herself Tonantzin, but rather, the "Ever-Virgin Holy Mary." The Virgin continues to identify herself as the Mother of God by using terms derived from traditional religion. The first reference, "Dios Teotl," grafts Spanish and Nahuatl words for "God" into a single term, followed by native designations for the ultimate deity: "the One through Whom We Live," "the Creator of Persons," "the Owner of What is Near and Together," "the Lord of Heaven and Earth."

The association with Tonantzin, however, comes up at another pivotal moment. After Juan Diego has attempted to avoid her to fetch a priest for his dying uncle, the Virgin sends him back to the summit of Tepeyac to gather the roses that will (unbeknownst to Juan Diego) be accompanied by the painting on his *tilma* as the sign for the bishop. The miraculous sign must come from Tepeyac, the home of Tonantzin.[12] A natural spring with healing waters was said to flow at the site where the first structure was built in her honor.

The Virgin's message, that she desires a hermitage, a home, a temple at Tepeyac (these three different words are used in progression), establishes her place among all those who dwell in New Spain. But while she makes herself known as mother of Spanish, *mestizo*, and *mulatto* Christians alike, it is Juan Diego who must deliver her message. In the apparition of Our Lady of Guadalupe to an indigenous convert, the Mother of God gently but firmly makes known her maternity of the native inhabitants of the American continent. The revelation is placed not in the hands of the ecclesial institution, but in those of a *macehual*, a farm laborer. A catechist from a newly evangelized people is sent to a bishop-elect of the Office of the Spanish Inquisition. A convert makes known the will of God to the official teaching authority of the local church. It is a stunning usurpation, an unambiguous overturning of Spanish triumphalism.

The Guadalupan devotion, then, serves as a fitting "container" for the fervor of new immigrants in the North. As a recognizable national symbol, the Virgin is capable of uniting Mexicans from diverse states of origin and of bringing together Mexican nationals and Mexican-Americans. The dialogue of the story allows for non-Mexicans to participate in the devotion as well. But the surety with which adherents can be convinced of her maternal care extends to the origins of the devotion itself. Through image and narrative, Our Lady of Guadalupe has been known—has been *seen* and *met*—by believers marginalized here in the United States or in their home countries.

Virgilio Elizondo points out that with the Conquest, native nations were subjugated on their own soil; Juan Diego Cuauhtlatoatzin found himself an alien in his own homeland. His figure provides a compelling model for those who must establish their own place in a new civic and ecclesial setting. The Virgin herself illumines the way.

* * * * *

Mexicans in Newburgh had been celebrating an annual Guadalupan celebration in a parish for more than two decades when the adaptation of a popular custom from Mexico added an electrifying element to the December twelfth observance. The *Carrera Antorcha Guadalupana*, Guadalupan Torch Relay, brought to our parish (and to many others in the archdiocese) a torch from Mexico City lit from the flame tended in the basilica.

If bicycle pilgrimages to Juquila are typical of Oaxacan devotion to its favorite virgin, the *Antorcha* is a tradition beloved to Puebla and its neighbors.[13] Back home, many of the sending communities of Mexican immigrants in New York organize yearly pilgrimages in which relay runners carry a lit torch from the basilica to their hometowns in Mexico. Passed from hand to hand as runners relieve one another, a human chain delivers the torch, carried entirely by foot, to its destination. The New York adaptation of this custom had the *Carrera Antorcha* arrive at St. Patrick's Cathedral, where delegations of runners came to light a torch to carry back to their local parishes.

The organization that directs the Guadalupan Torch Relay, *La Asociación Tepeyac* (the Tepeyac Association)—a federation of some forty local Mexican committees in New York's metropolitan area—was begun in 1997 in a church basement in the South Bronx. A year previously, the Jesuit order had sent one of its brothers (a native of Zacatecas studying in Chicago at the time) to New York to assess the needs of the burgeoning Mexican population.[14] Funded by the Jesuits and backed by the chancery office, the Tepeyac Association began providing a range of services, including information and the coordination of grassroots organizing efforts for recently arrived Mexican migrants and immigrants.

Over the years the organization's efforts, especially with regard to difficult matters such as deportations or labor abuses, earned for it the trust of diverse immigrant communities. After September 11, Tepeyac staff members became the principal spokespersons for the families of undocumented immigrants (not only Mexicans) who had died or disappeared at the World Trade Center.[15] Through the Association, immigrants and their supporters have lobbied for changes in

A runner in New York
carries the torch brought from
the Basilica of St. Mary of Guadalupe

national policies (e.g., a legalization program) as well as state policies (e.g., vehicular licenses for undocumented drivers). The organization's signature achievement, however, has been the Torch Relay, which enacts the Virgin of Guadalupe's crossing the border.

Thanks to the efforts of another of Newburgh's Mexican founding families, runners from our parish have taken part in the *Antorcha* since its inception. The Tepeyac Association has carried out some form of the *Antorcha* since 1998. In their first meetings in our church basement, founding members from Puebla expressed their desire to import this tradition from their homeland. Their reasoning was simple: if every year *antorchas* are brought to the villages of the Virgin's devotees, why shouldn't they be delivered to emigrant communities here?

Beginning as a relay going simply from St. Patrick's Cathedral to local parishes, the route of the *Antorcha* soon expanded. During its first two years, the *Antorcha* met tremendous immediate response. Mexican communities in New York enthusiastically recruited runners. Mexico's best known rock-and-roll band granted permission for the Tepeyac Association to adopt its ode to "*la Virgen Morena*," "the Dark Virgin," for the Torch Relay. A route would be set up months in advance and teams would take responsibility for predetermined legs of the arduous journey.

The response reverberated just as resoundingly in Puebla, and quickly thereafter in neighboring states, where sending communities asked to receive the torch before it made its way north. The situation

faced by undocumented immigrants and their families had been growing more and more dire since September 11 as, simultaneously, efforts
for national legislative reform were proving futile. Immigrant communities needed hope. In 2002, affirmed by the new archbishop who
pledged his support of a bi-national relay, the Tepeyac Association expanded the *Antorcha*'s route on both sides of the border.

Sending communities usually host the runners and other pilgrims
of the *Antorcha* in parishes (often with Mass, in order to properly receive the visit of the blessed images of the Virgin and St. Juan Diego
Cuauhtlatoatzin that accompany runners and the lit torch). Local
supporters take turns bearing the torch, knowing that the same flame
will eventually reach their children, friends, spouses, or neighbors in
the North. In one town in Puebla, so many runners came out that organizers had to limit participation to those who themselves had been
migrants.

Before crossing the border with the lit torch, runners carry it
through several southern states that send emigrants to New York—
Guerrero, Hidalgo, Morelos, Veracruz, Tlaxcala, Puebla—and into
the northern mountains of Oaxaca. Leaving the Federal District, runners make the grueling trip north through the State of Mexico and
Tamaulipas. On the northern side of the border, the *Antorcha* passes
through fourteen states—almost all of which are new receiving states
for Mexican immigration. Currently, the Torch Relay covers some four
thousand miles in approximately seventy days, and in 2005 included
over seven thousand participants—mostly young people—on both
sides of the border.

One of my teenage students from our parish catechism program
had this to say about her participation in the Torch Relay:

> I felt shivers when I took it [the *Antorcha*] in my hand, be-
> cause I started to think about all the people in Mexico who
> held this same torch before it got up here. I was wondering if
> maybe my grandmother and the people in my town had
> touched it. Even if they didn't it is still special, because I
> know it went through there. But mostly I ran because of *la
> Virgen*. She is always there for me, even when I don't have
> enough faith or if I do something wrong, I know she is
> watching me. I just kept thinking about her and running and
> running and I felt like she was giving me energy, I never ran

like that before. It's like, I wanted to say thank you to her and ask her to keep taking care of my family.

In Mexico, the *Antorcha* is a religious and cultural custom; in the North, this tradition takes on an added element: political resistance. Runners routinely make a stop at the White House to protest for immigration reform. Even as illegal immigration from Mexico has leveled off, reaching a plateau in mid-2006, raids on workplaces have increased dramatically—intensifying the air of fear and uncertainty in immigrant communities.

Participants carry the lit torch not only to manifest their devotion to Our Lady of Guadalupe, but also to proclaim a contemporary version of her message. In a single, symbolic act, runners make visible the Mexican and Mexican-American presence in the North. The *Antorcha* not only brings light, it also sheds light on the plight of undocumented immigrants. The forming of a human, mobile chain defies the border that divides families and separates sending and receiving migrant communities.

In the Northeast, the torch has represented the determination on the part of Mexican Catholics to have local parishes and civil authorities recognize their presence. When bringing the *Antorcha* to their parishes and neighborhoods, organizers had to approach local church and municipal authorities; for many, this meant coming into contact for the first time with the larger social or ecclesial structures where they now lived. Like Juan Diego Cuauhtlatoatzin, who transgressed socio-political and cultural-religious boundaries in delivering the Virgin's words and image to the bishop, runners of the *Antorcha* become the Virgin's emissaries, "messengers for the dignity of a single people divided by the border."[16]

A congratulatory message from the Vatican delivered in honor of the *Antorcha*'s lighting at the basilica in 2007 framed the tradition's new symbolism with these words: the torch represents "the light of faith which illumines the daily struggle" of those "forced to live difficult situations as migrants and immigrants." The papal communiqué coming from the highest authority in the church lauds the efforts of modern-day Mexican immigrants, as Juan Diego Cuauhtlatoatzin eventually gained the approval of the Spanish bishop.

A press release issued by the Tepeyac Association upon the *Antorcha*'s culmination in 2005 stated that "for the first time, the Torch

Relay has been very well received in the City of New York."[17] The Cathedral had "opened wide its doors" and allowed the *Antorcha* and two accompanying images to be carried right up to the main altar. Municipal authorities cooperated amicably—and even blocked off additional streets. These were "signs" that Mexicans were finally being accepted, an acceptance that came about, at least in part, *because of* the Guadalupan Torch Relay in which the Virgin crosses the border each year, illumined by the torch that announces her coming.

Though *guadalupanos* believe that the Virgin Mary is always present, there is something electrifying about seeing the image cross over. Without adaptations of traditional customs like the *Antorcha*, believers "fall asleep" to her presence. As in the apparition story in which the Virgin interrupts Juan Diego Cuauhtlatoatzin's journey, she continues actively to seek her children's gaze. It is as if she must find a way to catch their attention—braving any barrier—to arrive wherever they are.

In 2002—the first year the runners crossed the border—the organizers of the *Antorcha* in Newburgh lent us a video that we watched with a roomful of immigrant friends. The footage depicted confusion at the border, where federal agents were not quite sure what to make of the pedestrians in jogging suits (and one in a Roman collar), a caravan of vehicles, two huge framed images surrounded by candles and, of course, the flaming torch. Officials conferred amongst themselves, shaking their heads. The highway scenery and glaring streetlights did not provide a pious ambience, but then again, this was no typical procession. Watching the video, even though we knew already what the outcome would be, our own tension was palpable.

After some time, the band of runners was finally given authorization to cross over. Vigor and voice gathered against the stark backdrop of the pilgrimage, now more of a march. Runners hoisted the images of the Virgin of Guadalupe and of Juan Diego Cuauhtlatoatzin and thrust the *antorcha* high into the evening sky, singing *La Guadalupana* on the open highway. I looked around at the others in the room. We all had tears coursing down our faces: she had crossed.

The Virgin crosses borders even when her devotees cannot. Undocumented immigrants and their families live in a state of exile in the North, where, ironically, the tightening of the border has kept "in" many migrants who would otherwise have gone home for visits (and might have remained). The years trapped in this state of limbo (immortalized by Los Tigres del Norte in their ballad "*La Jaula de Oro*," "The Golden Cage") weaken emigrants' ties to their sending communities and reduce their chances of returning home.

Families of undocumented immigrants are separated, with no reunion in sight. One of the most challenging pastoral situations my husband and I face is when undocumented immigrants' parents die back home, and their adult children are unable to attend their funerals because, to return to their own families, they would have to risk crossing the border illegally again.

Having made *compadrazgos* (relationships centered on the bond between godparents and godchildren) in New York, my husband and I occasionally visit families of our godchildren in Mexico. These visits have been immensely instructive, but also inevitably painful. Each time we travel to these sending communities, we note two substantial changes: improvements in the standard of living (more vehicles, plumbing, electricity, paved roads) and fewer young people. Disproportionately in the rural sector, local economies have become dependent on the exportation of the workforce: it is the exodus of their future.

Regions like the area around Tehuitzingo have come to rely on an artificial economy based on the remittances sent back home by its emigrants. In 1996, remittances to Mexico amounted to four billion dollars. Within ten years, they had soared to over 20 billion, making up a staggering portion of the country's national revenues. Most years, remittances come second only to petroleum.

And then there are the collective remittance projects such as those depicted in *La Sexta Seccion*, "The Sixth Neighborhood." This award-winning documentary about a campaign by migrants from Puebla living in Newburgh chronicles efforts to raise more than $100,000 for various projects in their home village.

The documentary ends by highlighting the group's most ambitious plan: to collect funds for a well to solve the village's drastic water shortage. One member of the group explained to my husband and me that while their previous projects had improved the village's quality of life, their ultimate goal was to make it possible for future generations to stay home, instead of emigrating.

But will they be able to? Small-scale traditional farming is fading as a viable livelihood for families who have no other source of income. U.S. dollars being sent back home often help pay for young people's studies; however, there is no guarantee that a diploma will secure a job. (One Mexican friend of ours refers to his country's institutions of higher learning as "unemployment factories.")

One year, I wrote with glee to my anthropologist friend in Mexico about our successful December twelfth celebration in Newburgh. Her response saddened me: "I am happy for you, but my heart cries, because the more our people establish their *fiestas* in the North, the less likely they will be to come home."

In the North, Latinos have revitalized the inner city of Newburgh with the establishment of small businesses, investment in struggling neighborhoods, and participation in the work force. In settled populations—now more *im*migrant than migrant—a shift has taken place. Undocumented immigrants who are eligible to do so complete the lengthy and complicated task of procuring legal status. Families apply for mortgages and buy houses. The stubborn goal of return (among migrants, "next year, in December" is repeated like the refrain of the chosen people in the diaspora), for some, is realized. For most, like the family of the teenager who described running with the *Antorcha*, it has been transformed into an acceptance of the reality that the land of exile has become home.

Mexicans in New York City recently took the lead in the city's Latino birth rate (the birth rate of Mexicans in New York also recently surpassed the birth rate of their compatriots in Mexico). An article in the *New York Times* reported that there were 350,000 Mexicans and Mexican-Americans living in the metropolitan area, qualifying this as a "conservative" figure; community organizers estimate that the population will soon reach half a million, if it has not already. The priest with whom my husband and I work comes from a diocese in Jalisco whose numbers are lower than the number of Mexicans in the archdiocese of New York.

One sociologist who has studied Mexican emigration in depth believes that Mexican-American identity is still being established; the influx is so recent that Mexicans are still figuring out what it means to be Mexican in New York. In Newburgh, an up-and-coming generation of Mexican leaders harbors no illusions about going back. Their children, the city's first Mexican-Americans, navigate their own course between two languages and two cultural worlds. Like Juan Diego Cuauhtlatoatzin, they stand between two radically different realities. As a bridge that connects the religious practices of their families' past and the new *mestizaje* that is their future, the Virgin of Guadalupe will be discovered yet again through their eyes.

* * * * *

Losing sight of and rediscovering the foundational story is such a recurring theme in Guadalupan history that it might be considered an integral part of the devotion itself. During the 1920s, a Mexican Jesuit driven from his homeland by the Cristero persecutions[18] to seek refuge in the North made an unexpected discovery in New York City. While doing research in the archives of the public library, he came across fragments of a Nahuatl document relating the Guadalupan apparition.[19] The text, shorter and less detailed than the *Nican Mopohua*, concurs with the central plot of its better-known counterpart, in which a Spanish bishop is confronted with the testimony of an indigenous convert to whom the Virgin Mary has appeared, and through whom she leaves her mysterious, miraculous image "as luster for all the world."

Much about the devotion's origins remain, even now, elusive.[20] In hindsight almost five centuries later, it seems that the Guadalupan apparition was woven seamlessly into two millennia of Marian veneration. However, a closer look reveals that the devotion's "crossing over" from a marginal native memory to a universally embraced tradition was somewhat more complicated.

The first recipient of Our Lady of Guadalupe's gaze, "the littlest of [her] children," slipped from history's view not once but twice. The encounter of St. Juan Diego Cuauhtlatoatzin with the Virgin Mary was preserved in Nahuatl oral narratives and indigenous codices preserved by native Christians in the Tepeyac area. As a popular, non-official tradition either unknown or not credible to Spanish prelates, it might have been lost had it not been for the nationalistic interests of Guadalupan advocates a century later.

In 1648, the story of the Guadalupan apparitions was put into writing for the first time, more than one hundred years after the encounters were supposed to have taken place. Older documents, including indigenous annals, had made reference to the apparitions, but up until then, none had described them in detail. Embellished with biblical and patriotic interpretation, the new text made a huge impact on Mexicans of Spanish descent born in the Americas. A year later, a different redactor—the proctor of the sanctuary—published a more

meticulous account in a version transcribed and translated by edu-
cated bilingual Nahuas (the now-definitive *Nican Mopohua*, contained in the *Huey Tlamahuicoltica* or "Great Happening"). Miguel
Sánchez and Luis Laso de la Vega, respectively, both *criollos* and both
priests, credited as their source an independent indigenous tradition
about which they learned from natives living near the sanctuary.

The circulation of these texts describing the apparitions for the
first time coincided with the nascent desire of Mexican-born
Spaniards to gain independence from Spain. The role of the Virgin of
Guadalupe in the development of *criollo* consciousness has been well
documented. I would rather highlight the uncomfortable fact that
until relatively recently, Juan Diego Cuauhtlatoatzin was given surprisingly minimal attention in official discourse surrounding the
newly recovered foundational narrative.

Historian Stafford Poole, in his exhaustive investigation into the origins of the Guadalupan devotion from 1531 to 1797, surveyed sermons
after the publication of Sánchez's highly patriotic version (favored over
the *Nican Mopohua*). His research reveals that while much was made of
the Virgin of Guadalupe (the "second Eve" in the New World), astoundingly little was made of her emissary: with only a few exceptions,
most homilists omitted Juan Diego Cuauhtlatoatzin's name.

(In a contemporary twist fitting to this retelling of the Guadalupan story, preparations for the 2002 canonization of Blessed Juan
Diego Cuauhtlatoatzin sparked controversy: detractors argued that as
a historical figure, Juan Diego never existed. The heated debate even
led to the dismissal of the basilica's rector when a letter he had co-
written to the Vatican on the eve of the canonization expressing concern over insufficient historical investigation was leaked to the press.)

In promoting the devotion among their peers and seeking increasingly higher levels of approbation by the hierarchical church,
criollos marginalized Juan Diego's role, overlooking for a second time
the contribution of the indigenous evangelizer to whom the devotion
owes its existence. In the first instance, silence regarding Juan Diego
Cuauhtlatoatzin may be attributed to Spanish ignorance of an indigenous oral tradition; the second instance, however, rendered him invisible in plain sight. By negating the content of the apparition story—
in which an Indian is chosen to bear the Virgin's word and
person—the sense of election is extended only to the *criollos*.

From its beginning, Guadalupanismo has contained two currents: a populist devotion belonging to the indigenous Christians around Tepeyac who preserved the memory of an indigenous evangelizer; and an official one corresponding to the *criollos* who controlled the sanctuary. The Nahuatl text discovered in the New York Public Library—like the *Nican Mopohua*, based on oral tradition—names neither Juan Diego nor the bishop; and in an ironic reversal, the popular song *La Guadalupana* names Juan Diego but does not even mention the bishop!

Here we arrive at the heart of the dilemma. Were the apparition stories invented as a ploy by Spanish missionaries? The most celebrated Mexican religious customs are hybrids propagated by clergy, hybrids in which, following a centuries-old technique sanctioned by papal approval, missionaries substituted Christian customs for pagan ones (e.g., *las Posadas* replaced an annual Festival of Light in honor of Huitzilopochtli at the time of the winter solstice).

Or were the real protagonists the indigenous converts who sought to "baptize" pre-existent practices as a defense against the new religion being forced upon them? (The cross, after all, arrived with the sword, and a brief early experiment of inter-religious dialogue between Franciscans and native religious leaders had ended miserably.) This syncretistic approach, while recognizing the agency of native people falls short of recognizing their Christianity. *Los Días de los Muertos*, the Days of the Dead, for example, are frequently touted as purely pre-Hispanic, as if five centuries of celebration had nothing to do with the universal church's observance of All Saints' and All Souls' Days.

The true miraculousness of the devotion's origins lies in the cultivation of the gospel by indigenous Christians. The Virgin of Guadalupe "appeared" in the religious thought and practice of the Nahua people. She spoke their language, idiomatically and symbolically, inviting them to become her partners in the New Creation. In time the official church, like the bishop, gave its approval by authenticating devotion to the Virgin of Guadalupe.

For all its cultural complexity and historical ambiguity, the Guadalupan story encodes a historical process told in symbolic language. The evangelization of the Americas hinged upon the collaboration of native Christians (like the anonymous Chatino catechist of Amialtepec who promoted devotion to the Virgin Mary around

Juquila). These committed converts proclaimed their new faith to indigenous communities in the context of the extreme social and spiritual displacement of the Conquest. Contrary to *criollo* interpretation, Our Lady of Guadalupe did not appear to the nation state of Mexico, but rather, to the first *peoples* of the Americas.

Virgilio Elizondo notes that although the Virgin identified herself using specifically indigenous theological terms, when Juan Diego took her message to the bishop, even though she had not identified herself as such, he named her unequivocally as "the Mother of our Savior, Jesus Christ." It was a resounding indigenous confession of faith.

During the Papal Inquiry of 1666, prompted by the petition for the designation of a formal feast day with its own Mass and office in honor of Our Lady of Guadalupe, proponents of the devotion interviewed indigenous and Spanish witnesses. The interviews, which confirm the existence of an oral tradition honoring the memory of Juan Diego Cuauhtlatoatzin, were revisited as primary sources during investigation of the case for his canonization. Nahuatl-speakers recalled a celebration in which the bishop, together with indigenous Christians who performed ceremonial dances to the accompaniment of drum and flute music, delivered an image in procession to the chapel at Tepeyac with St. Juan Diego Cuauhtlatoatzin present.

The interviews and other ancient sources present a composite portrayal of a devout caretaker of the first Guadalupan hermitage, a man with a reputation for holiness who evangelized other indigenous converts through his testimony to the apparitions.[21] It was recorded that the saying, "May God be as good to you as he was to Juan Diego" was used as a greeting or blessing among native Christians. Multiple sources testified that farming communities often visited him to ask him to pray on their behalf for good harvests.

While apparitions during the Conquest and colonial period demonstrate a common symbolic structure, a characteristic that all recognized Marian apparitions—whether ancient, medieval, or contemporary—seem to share is that they take place in populations experiencing social stress. The extreme duress on the native population in New Spain in the years immediately following the Conquest is summarized in this sobering account from 1582: "Many Indians hang themselves, others let themselves die of hunger, others poison themselves with herbs; there are mothers who kill the children to whom they have just given birth, saying they do so in order to spare them from the suffering they are forced to endure."[22] Other records tell of entire ethnic groups committing collective suicide by drastically curtailing their birth rates. The decimation of the native population by epidemics is alluded to by the illness that threatens to take the life of Juan Bernardino, Juan Diego's uncle.

The basic premise of contemporary theological interpretations of Our Lady of Guadalupe holds that only a symbol formulated in intelligible native terms and communicated through maternal reproductive imagery could address the dire situation of indigenous Christians who had lost the will to live.

In native theology, *xochitl en cuicatl*, flower and song, express ultimate truth. The narrative that begins with the song of birds ("The Eagle Who Sings" hears their melody as he approaches the summit) ends with flowers, roses gathered in the *tilma*. Christian revelation takes the form of a tiny, four-petalled flower placed directly over the Virgin's slightly swelling belly. The anatomy of her figure is accentu-

Runners in La Noria Hidalgo, Puebla, finish their village's annual torch relay

Traditional dancers in Puebla perform in honor of the Virgin of Guadalupe

ated by the position of her right thigh, which helps viewers to grasp
the significance of the flower's placement.

Tucked inconspicuously into the vine-and-leaf pattern, the *nav
ollin*, the Nahua center of the universe, can be found in her womb.
Instead of the fierce and bloodthirsty Huitzilopochtli (who, flanked
by two identically shaped round petals, glares from the center of the
huge stone artifact we now call the Aztec Calendar), the New Era—
the Sixth Sun—dawns in the Virgin's image. The New Creation is
found in a tiny child held in the cradle of her womb. Juan Diego
Cuauhtlatoatzin's confession of faith finds its visual counterpart:
Christ has arrived in the Americas.

✳ ✳ ✳ ✳ ✳

For seven years, a mission project in the Mid-Hudson River Valley has
carried a traveling image of the Virgin of Guadalupe to the most mar-

ginalized Spanish-speaking communities in the region. Like the one in our parish, the framed reproduction of the *tilma* was brought from the basilica itself; but unlike the image that graces our church building, this one was destined to keep traveling.

In many of the areas of Mexico that send migrants to our area, local communities rotate the hosting of a Mass, procession, and celebratory meal on the twelfth of each month in honor of the Virgin of Guadalupe's apparition. An image of the Virgin "visits" each place. The missionary priest we worked with suggested that we begin practicing the same custom. Oftentimes, the visits take place in pockets among the most "invisible" populations of the Hudson Valley, namely, *guadalupanos* among the Spanish-speaking inmates in prison and among the seasonal farm workers in apple orchards and corn fields. Through my husband's work with agricultural laborers on some forty farms, we had met numerous Spanish-speaking harvesting crews and year-round families who were new to the area. Migrant communities, not yet integrated into local churches, find in a devotion centered on a sacred image a spirituality that can travel—and that can sustain them while their roots are adjusting to new soil.

During the first years of the mission, finding a place for the monthly observance in areas where there are Latino migrants and immigrants but no church services in Spanish was challenging. In these places, the Hispanic *presence* is still "invisible" even though its *numbers* are not. One parish priest in a town with a growing Latino population wondered at our visit, since there were "hardly any" Spanish speakers there. In another town, hundreds of signatures on petitions gathered by Latino Catholics have not convinced the pastor of the need for a weekly Spanish Mass. One organizer complained, "Now I knew how Juan Diego felt, returning day after day to the bishop's palace."[23]

For me, the mission became a way to integrate into the familiar area around my hometown the spirituality my husband and I had experienced abroad. Music sets the tone for our celebrations. A young musician (from the town of the documentary about the remittance projects) leads traditional Marian songs (*La Guadalupana, Buenos Días Paloma Blanca, Santa María del Camino, Mi Virgen Ranchera, Quien es esa estrella, Adios, Reina del Cielo*). When Mass is said, music for the entire liturgy is drawn from songs familiar to people from rural Latin America. The climax of the celebration comes both at the consecration and at the memorial acclamation, the *a capella* singing of the *Bendito* of their ancestors, which most migrants have not heard since leaving home.[24]

On one visit, we met a farm worker who was new to a crew that we had known for many years. (Nineteen members of this crew had just been picked up while driving to an orchard to harvest apples, and while they awaited deportation in a detention center, new workers arrived to take their places.) The farm worker's battered sneakers were held together with string instead of shoelaces, and his well-worn clothes were too light for New York's chilly nights. He had just come from North Carolina, where he had worked picking peaches. Before that, he had worked in Florida harvesting citrus fruits. A member of the church choir at home, he confessed that he had not attended Mass (or held a guitar) for two years—since losing his coffee farm in Veracruz, where his wife and daughters still lived.

He cradled a borrowed guitar fondly, and at the first strum it became immediately apparent that we were in the presence of a bona fide musician. A few soulful riffs and a gruff voice combined to produce a masterful Mexican version of the blues. After having been so long deprived of a familiar religious setting, he sat now before the image of the Virgin of Guadalupe. As he tuned the strings, limbering his fingers, I wondered, what would be the first song he sang? Surely the lyrics of the hymn he chose would tell of his situation. Would they decry injustice, or express longing and nostalgia? The simplicity of the song that spontaneously came to him took my breath away:

> We have come to this place to worship the Lord
> We have come to this place to worship the Lord
> I thank You for all You do,
> for all You have done
> and for all You will do.[25]

After singing this psalm of unconditional praise, followed by a traditional Guadalupan hymn, he put the guitar aside and we prayed a rosary for all migrants and their families. The next day, there would be calls placed seeking legal counsel for the detainees and coats found for the new arrivals. But for that night, there was just prayer, prayer at the feet of the Virgin.

During the Fourth Mexican Workshop on Migrant Ministry, a scripture scholar noted that during migration, faith grows; it is insti-

tutional accompaniment that is often lacking. The biblical root
metaphors of exodus and exile come sharply into relief as dispossessed
people seek the divine across borders. Where new immigrants are not
yet integrated into local congregations, the presence of a meaningful
image can become a central medium for religious experience. Displacement heightens, it does not diminish, the power of that image.
The face of a maternal symbol lends even more comfort when it is con-
templated far from home. And a song that unequivocally praises a God
who works wonders—even while believers cannot yet see the evidence—
speaks of great faith.

The lyrics of the farm worker's song sounded to me like a modern day version of the Magnificat:

My soul proclaims the greatness of the Lord,
My spirit rejoices in God my Savior.
The Almighty has done great things for me
Holy is God's name.

In St. Luke's gospel, the evangelist places a Christian hymn modeled on Hannah's Song (1 Samuel 2:1–10) on the Virgin Mary's lips.
A young girl pregnant with the unborn Christ proclaims the Magnificat while on a journey. The narrative presents an unwed teenager
who has just traveled through her people's occupied homeland not
knowing whether her betrothed will accept her pregnancy, whether
the liberation about which she sings will ever be achieved, or whether
this child will bring her joy or grief. Mary of Nazareth relies on God
completely and wholeheartedly—even as she stands on the threshold
of an uncertain future.

The visits of the traveling image of the Virgin of Guadalupe, the
Misión Guadalupana, give expression to this experience. The mission's root metaphor echoes the great biblical motifs of exodus and
exile while its methodology incorporates basic elements of Latin
American popular religious practice: the traveling image that journeys
from place to place; the role of the hosts, comparable to that of *may-
ordomos*; and pilgrimage in miniature—the procession.

Albeit on a much smaller scale compared to the way this practice is
carried out in their sending communities, the procession creates a sense
of familiarity and belonging. When winter snows move the celebration
indoors, devotees still find a way to enact this beloved custom, for car-

rying lit candles into the dusk while walking together in procession behind the beloved, traveling image forms the heart of the mission. In its
new setting in the North, the procession takes on new meaning, retrac-
ing the steps of those who came across the border into this new land.

Typically, a request to receive the Virgin comes from devotees in
order to offer a prayer intention. In one particularly wrenching visit,
we brought the Virgin to a family from a Zapotec-speaking village in
Oaxaca. Four family members (a father in his late thirties, his son, his
son-in-law, and his nephew) had been lost while attempting to cross
the border. The son-in-law and nephew, both teenagers, had died of
dehydration and their bodies had been found; the father and son were
still missing.

In a situation such as this, the presence of the Virgin's image gives
more consolation than words.

Not all visits mourn a tragedy; some celebrate a housewarming,
or express thanks for a favor received through the Virgin's intercession. Hosts invite relatives, friends, acquaintances, and neighbors, and
toward the end of the gathering, serve refreshments—for, as at a patronal feast in a home village, the celebration would not be complete
without having everyone eat together. The image stays with the family or community for the month, and on the twelfth of the next
month, the hosts deliver the image to the next place.

When the Guadalupan Mission began, the exchange between
guadalupanos in different locations connected Spanish-speaking newcomers, not only providing information about local parishes but also
facilitating access to social services or workers' compensation, participation in marches for immigrants' rights, or the arranging of collec-
tions and funerary services. Typically, responses are generous and immediate when the body of a migrant or immigrant is sent home.
Organizers fan out into factories and stores bearing a photo of the de-
ceased. The thousands of dollars required are gathered quickly, donated by immigrants motivated by the saying, "Today it is them, to-
morrow it could be me."

The monthly gatherings include the recitation of the rosary—
complete with traditional hymns and prayers between each decade,
three adaptations of the Hail Mary,[26] and the Litany of Loretto at the
end. The words of the "Hail, Holy Queen" come alive among migrant and immigrant communities in the Hudson River Valley in a

way I have never before experienced. Physical geography itself lends a literal quality to the prayer:

> To thee do we send up our sighs, mourning and weeping in this valley of tears. Turn then, O most gracious advocate, thine eyes of mercy toward us, and after this our exile, show unto us the blessed fruit of thy womb, Jesus.

Simple, spontaneous offerings repeated over the first year made the journeying image truly *ours*. During those initial months, receiving families or communities decorated the image as if to leave an imprint of their encounter with the Virgin. First, a tiny rosary of white beads on a gold chain was dangled over one corner of the frame by a family whose son had been shot and killed by a gang. Next, an artificial red rose was taped onto the picture by a mother whose daughter had been born with medical complications. A scapular was hung in thanksgiving for a safe border crossing. A small plastic cross was taped onto a corner by farm workers from the corn camp where a young Mayan had drowned. Artificial green vines were affixed to the bottom of the picture, creating a verdant bed, by the family of a seven-year-old who had died of leukemia. A more humble offering—gift bows attached to the frame—came from the apple farm whose nineteen workers had been deported by Immigration.

Even if devotees cannot make the pilgrimage to the Virgin's basilica, they can still stand in her sanctuary, for wherever her image is—in trailer parks, jails, in packing houses, or in tortilla factories—there she herself is. Anywhere can serve as her sanctuary. The task falls upon believers precisely *to make a place for her*. She has journeyed all this way to entrust them with her message: to build a hermitage...a house...a church where she can, once again, appear.

A traveler bearing our individual and collective joys and sorrows in her very person, the Virgin of Guadalupe gathers us into the folds of her timeless, starry mantle. An anchoring presence, she steadies us on our individual journeys and brings us back—for wherever one's mother is, home can be found. Reflected in her loving eyes, we see ourselves for who we truly are. Though far from where our lives began, we are no longer lost. Her tender gaze gives us the courage to continue the pilgrimage of our daily lives.

An altar made of planks set between two trailers, carefully adorned with a white cloth and fresh flowers from the orchards...the sun setting in the background...the scent of perfume and shampoo as farm workers assemble, freshly showered and changed after a long workday...the heartfelt music led by a choir. *Everybody* sings...children (including my own) running and playing amidst the trees...the birds adding their songs to the celebration...and, most of all, the majestic, comforting, infinitely alluring beauty of her image. St. Juan Diego Cuauhtlatoatzin's words come to me: "Am I dreaming?"

In the company of other devotees, I, too, have come home. In improvised sanctuaries the Virgin keeps her promise to "reveal and give all her love, compassion, help and defense." I see the icon for what it is—a window—and she appears. I *see* her.

Like a mother who guards the exact memory of her children's first steps, the precise timbre of their laugh, or their first words, the Virgin of Guadalupe remembers. She remembers the *haciendas* in the Mixteca, the falling bottom of the agricultural market, the relatives lost in the desert. She treasures each attempt to sight her presence in a new landscape. She watches over those who have been left behind, as well as over every migrant's step. She sees. She remembers.

The one who is herself a traveler has known immense suffering, and has come through to the other side. Hers is not an unchallenged, comfortable mother's love, but an unconditional, passionate commitment from a woman who has *given life* in the middle of genocide and death. As the Virgin Mary "saved" Christianity from irrelevance at the time of the Conquest by making the new religion both fathomable and attractive to indigenous converts, in many areas of the North, *Guadalupanismo* has saved dominant-culture Catholicism from being too foreign or too forbidding to Latin American immigrants.

The narrative of the Guadalupan story is defined by boundaries, the transgression of which provides the basic content of its plot. The Virgin crosses these boundaries in order to grace us with her presence and to witness her children's daily journeys. A repository of memory, she has a gaze that is powerful enough to lift whole communities from obscurity. She guards episodes in history that might otherwise be forgotten. In the simple fact of their *being seen*, a redemptive process has already begun.

A good mother, Our Lady of Guadalupe pushes her devotees beyond their own limited horizons of hope. She gives them herself; she shows them their true identities; and, in the communal dimension of the devotion, she gives them one another. This representation of the Virgin Mary also gives them her Son.

Like the verses of the Magnificat in which Mary sings that God "has brought down the powerful from their thrones, and lifted up the lowly" (Luke 1:52), the *Nican Mopohua* tells the story of salvation being accomplished, even when redemption is still too far off to see. The Virgin of Guadalupe is pregnant with a Son who changes the course of history. Every march, every Mass, every procession comes as a contraction bringing humanity one step closer to its eschatological destination, for the migrant phenomenon of our contemporary world is a biblical saga of epic proportions—the story of our times.

Here is the key to Judeo-Christian revelation; believing that salvation comes about in human history is, perhaps, the ultimate act of faith.

All Christian life is a passing over; our task is to waken from sleep. The scriptures teach us that we are all pilgrims on an exodus journey; Jesus leads us in a definitive crossing over. His mother comes to birth us into this, our true identity. When she appears, we are saved, for the "God-Bearer" does not come alone. The Virgin of Guadalupe is an icon of the divine presence, and the paschal mystery unfurls like a flower from her womb.

IV

Ruega por nosotros, Dolorosa
    Madre
Para que tu Hijo no nos
    desampare.

Pray for us,
    Sorrowful Mother,
That your Son not turn away
    from us.

✳ ✳ ✳ ✳ ✳ ✳ ✳ ✳ ✳ ✳ ✳

Los ángeles en el cielo
Te alaben con alegría
Y nosotros en la tierra
Digamos, "Ave Maria."

The angels in heaven
Laud you with joy
While we on earth
Your praises employ.

Más hermosa que la luna
Y más linda que el sol eres
Desde el principio del mundo
Señora bendita eres.

More beautiful than the moon
You shine more brightly than the sun
From the beginning of the world
You are blessed, holy one.

Del Oriente nace el sol
Dando al mundo hermosa luz
De tu boca nació el alba
Y de tu vientre, Jesús.

From the East, the sun is born
Giving light, dispelling doom
The dawn sprang from your mouth
And Jesus from your womb.

Y pues te coronaron
De diamantes y de flores
Te suplicamos Señora
Ruega por los pecadores.

And so You were crowned
With diamonds and flowers
We beseech You, Lady, pray
For sinners at all hours.

Nuestra Señora de la Soledad
Our Lady of Solitude

HER SILENCE, OUR SONG

* * * * * * * * * * * * *

María, Madre de gracia, Madre de misericordia
En la vida y en la muerte, ampáranos, Gran Señora.

Mary, Mother of grace, Mother of mercy,
Shelter us in life and in death, Great Lady.

— Traditional

From her magnificent baroque basilica, *la Virgen de la Soledad* (the Virgin of Solitude) presides over the city of Oaxaca, silently taking in the joys and sorrows of her subjects. Her constant presence has anchored the Archdiocese of Antequera and sea-faring devotees from the nearby state of Veracruz through the ebb and flow of four centuries. The city, in its frenetic growth, races through history around her. A tiny replica set into the outer wall of the church complex overlooks traffic rushing along the busy thoroughfare to the heart of the capital below.

Nowadays, she plays a rather ceremonial role, making an appearance at ecclesial or civic functions when duty calls. As patroness of the archdiocese, her image denotes *communitas* for Oaxaca; she is especially associated with the capital.

Like the basilica itself, which covers a subterranean vein of salt water, or the brocaded black robes that conceal the sparse image, the Virgin of Solitude obscures mystery in plain sight. A compass always there but seldom recognized, she is like the first star, which becomes visible only at dusk. Her beauty draws adherents to deeper waters. She provides clues to a hidden way, a mystic path. To truly encounter the Virgin of Solitude, I discovered, requires taking in the Passion that she perpetually witnesses.

* * * * *

The Soledad Basilica is arguably one of the most pleasant sites in the capital city. Although the streets above and below bustle with the frenzy of vehicles and pedestrians, the environs of the basilica provide a haven of space and beauty in the middle of urban congestion. The entire complex is constructed in Oaxaca's celebrated *cantera* stone (green with the exception of the façade, which is finished in yellow). In front of the sanctuary itself, a huge walled atrium creates a feeling of spaciousness, while just outside the gates the shady Garden of Socrates provides areas for cozy clusters of activity. Interspersed with the sheltering trees, along one side of the small plaza, four or five booths sell religious articles. In a corner, tables of regional sweets and pastries entice passersby. A stand offering traditional woven and embroidered clothing catches the eye. The stone fountain placed squarely in the center of the small plaza is surrounded by groupings of wrought iron tables and chairs, where Oaxacans and visitors alike can sit and enjoy the Soledad's famously refreshing *nieves*, flavored ices.

Next door to the basilica, the municipal offices of the capital city, housed in what used to be the convent of the church, are set around a stunningly beautiful courtyard. In the enormous open plaza, with rows and rows of stone steps leading to the street above, free cultural events for the public are held. And across from the plaza, the fine arts academy, Bellas Artes, with its own breathtaking architecture, provides a suitable setting for Oaxaca's new generations of artists and musicians who gather not only for classes but also to enjoy its bohemian ambience.

As the result of a serendipitous stroke of luck, my son started taking piano lessons in Bellas Artes, and so, twice a week, we would visit the Soledad. We would arrive as the heat of the day began to wind down and leave as the sun was setting in colors rivaling those of the phosphorescent flavored ices. With the basilica's baroque façade framed by palm trees in the foreground and a spectacular view of the mountains in the distance, lights would begin to appear one by one in the multitude of neighborhoods crowding the once-empty hills.

When I had made a first, obligatory visit to the Virgin herself (who is listed in every tourist guidebook), I thought she would never notice one more sightseer from her formidable gold pedestal. But I was surprised by the reaction she evoked from me. Passing the curious caged rock at the huge back doors and entering the basilica, I felt irresistibly drawn to the image—almost in spite of her ornate array. Her royal presence fills the echoing enormity of the baroque temple, pulling both the curious and the converted toward the altar.

Standing with her hands folded in a gesture of prayer, the Virgin is elevated on a gilded footstool, a life-sized statue behind a glass encasement. Her black velvet robes are embroidered with white lilies and encrusted in pearls. A gold band rims the pallor of her serene face. From her head, a black veil descends in sharp lines, forming a triangular mount of tranquility and perfection. She is gorgeous.

One single, luminous pearl glows on her smooth forehead; from her folded hands a jeweled rosary gracefully falls. The gold crown completes the costume. In case there was ever any doubt, the words etched in gold lettering on her glass chamber proclaim, "*Salve, Reina de Oaxaca*," "Hail, Queen of Oaxaca."

My critical mind asked how I could recognize in this Virgin's formidable stance the bent posture of a woman bowed with grief at her son's cross, or reconcile these ornate robes with the humble homespun tunic and veil of a village woman from Nazareth. But my heart and soul went out to her in a way I could not understand. She had something to tell me about life, and about *my* life. She seemed to speak to me.

Over the years, I visited the Virgin of Solitude often, even after my son lost his enthusiasm for the piano. Unlike the sanctuary at Juquila or the Basilica of the Virgin of Guadalupe—which overwhelm me with their sheer numbers of pilgrims—this church has a lonely feel to it, in keeping with its namesake and accentuated by the attire of the Virgin in mourning. Maybe it's the noise of the city in the background that heightens the sanctuary's hushed silence; perhaps it's the overdone baroque opulence, which stands in stark contrast to the poverty outside the gates. It definitely has to do with the solitary steps with which her adherents shuffle in to contemplate her sorrow and her serenity. The chandeliers perpetually held mid-air by a pair of life-sized angels, the richly gilded altar flanked by columns, the elaborate crown placed on the Virgin's head—none of these things can obscure her true identity behind the show of royal pageantry: she is the *Mater Dolorosa*, the sorrowing mother.

All day long, a steady, slow current of devotees streams in unob-
trusively, one by one, or in an occasional pair (a couple holding
hands, a grandmother and young grandson who finds the church entirely too quiet for his liking). Some arrive impeccably coiffed and
manicured; others wear the unmistakable garb of indigenous dress.
We are almost all women. We come seeking the same thing, to contemplate the Virgin's beauty from the pews, to gaze on her face—
though she does not look back (her set face is not sweetly inclined
like the Guadalupana's and, unlike the Juquilita, she averts her eyes).
She endures, patient and stiff in brocaded robes, tirelessly waiting for
us to come to her.

We are each alone with her, together. It's like having your
mother's undivided attention all for yourself, with the paradoxical certainty of knowing that your brothers and sisters have her attention
too. The hum of traffic outside melts into the quiet hush of the basilica; eyes adjust to the comforting, dim light of sanctuary. I imagine
that all of us would say we have been seen and heard. We are *all* her
favorite daughters.

In contemplating her beauty, devotees somehow regain their own
strength. We talk to her—out loud or, more often, in the silence of
our hearts—as we lay our troubles at her royal feet. A woman like us,
she understands. Sometimes we come to complain, sometimes to give
thanks, sometimes to cry. Once I witnessed a well-put-together middle-aged vendor with dignified bearing make her way to the altar. Arriving at the guard rail, she dissolved into tears, pouring out her soul
in a litany of confidences. After having delivered her discourse, she remained quietly on her knees for a moment, then dried her tears on
the hem of her dress. Drawing herself up to full height, she swiveled
on her heels to leave, just as composedly and determinedly as she had
entered.

My own interaction with the Virgin is not as dramatic. Some visits are purely mechanical—after all, this is just one thread in the fabric of my daily life, and Oaxaca lends itself to the frequent practice of
popular piety.

But at other times, when my mind circles like a hound with a hare
and I can't seem to clear my thoughts, she pulls me out of the tangle
of problems that I can't step out of on my own. Contemplating her
regal serenity, I am drawn to her. I raise my eyes and suddenly my vi-

sion clears: my emotions rise to the surface and I unburden my heart like a traveler unpacking. In her unmoving vigil, she accompanies me as I confront the uncomfortable truths of daily life—my kindergartner's recalcitrance over homework, the tedium of raising toddlers. My marriage comes sharply into focus.

With the Virgin of Solitude's steady presence to anchor me, I sink into deeper levels of reflection. My eldest daughter's changing body reminds me that I, too, am growing older. I look to the Virgin for clues. Not so much for the stereotypical qualities associated with the Virgin Mary, but for wisdom regarding how to be true to my vocation. For to truly follow one's vocation—whether it be motherhood or monasticism—requires a dying process, a certain letting go of expectations for one's own life.

And sometimes, living in Mexico, the outer world overwhelms me. With its poverty and political turmoil, Oaxaca also lends itself to public reasons for despair.

I don't have the strength to face it, but she does.

She stood at the foot of a cross and watched the life drain from her Son's body, cradled his broken corpse in a grotesque parody of the fondling of a newborn, grieved wordlessly over his senseless murder. And now, two thousand years later, she accompanies us, her other children, in our individual and collective miseries. Like the dutiful queen that she is, her person is intimately linked with the fate of the state. I have been told that in times of crisis in Oaxaca a *mancha* (a stain or spot) appears on her aristocratically white face.

The Virgin Mary's brocaded gown and gold crown remind believers that her humility and fidelity were rewarded lavishly. Injustice will *not* have the last say.

If she is a queen, it is because her subjects have made her one. We declared her sovereign. Perceiving in her silence a strength we do not possess, we recognize that we need her regal serenity.

I love her best when she is lowered down during Lent, when her ornate robes are traded for a plain black dress of mourning and the tall crown is exchanged for a simple circlet. Only once a year, for just three days preceding the Easter Vigil, the image is moved to a side area of the basilica floor.

As if she has waited all year for this moment, the Virgin of Solitude comes out from behind her glass barrier to a low platform lined with candles and positioned almost at our level. We cannot touch her, but her presence is so real, so near. If we were allowed, I suspect we would kiss her pale face, which now looks so gaunt. She is different, yet the same. Away from her throne, her erect posture bends. Her face changes, it becomes suddenly drawn. She appears older. When she comes closer, she reveals her true nature, destined to stand perpetually at the foot of a cross. *We* are the cause of her vigil now, the child to whom Christ pointed in John's gospel: "Mother, there is your son" (19:26). Bowed with grief for our sakes, she comes down from her throne; she shares our fate. She is truly one of us.

✻   ✻   ✻   ✻   ✻

According to legend, the Virgin of Soledad inaugurated her illustrious career as Oaxaca's patron under enigmatic circumstances. The foundational narrative, originally derived from oral tradition, was preserved in José Antonio Gay's *Historias de Oaxaca* (Histories of Oaxaca) and has been retold by contemporary chronicler Everardo Ramírez Bohórquez. On December 17, perhaps in the year 1620, a caravan of mule drivers en route from Veracruz to Guatemala camped on Campanario Mountain along the banks of the Atoyac River. The next day, they set out for Oaxaca before dawn. As light broke on the morning of December 18, the drivers suddenly realized that a mule they had never seen before was traveling along with the pack, carrying on her back a wooden chest (some versions say two chests). Fearing they might be accused of theft, the hired hands informed the owner of the mule train, who decided to turn over the animal and her cargo to the mayor in Oaxaca.

At around 9 AM, the caravan arrived at the outskirts of Oaxaca. The crew planned to rest and to eat their morning repast at the hermitage of St. Sebastian. The mule lay down on a huge rock near the hermitage, where she stayed throughout breakfast, and would not get up when it was time to leave. The drivers coaxed and beat the poor animal to no avail. They took the load off her back to relieve her fatigue. Someone set out to fetch the mayor. In the meantime, the mule, relieved of her burden, stood up, shook herself, took a couple of steps then fell down dead "as if struck by lightning."

At 11 AM, an entourage arrived—the mayor, his scribe, four other officials, and a host of curious onlookers. As if foreseeing the discovery's significance, the mayor, in a voice of authority, ordered the box to be opened and the scribe to take notes. The chest was laid on the rock. When it was opened, the gathered party discovered a three-foot tall, artfully carved statue of the Risen Christ and a delicate white face and pair of hands "like lilies." A written sign accompanied the find, bearing the words "The Most Blessed St. Mary of Solitude at the Foot of the Cross."[1]

The mayor, stating that the discovery fell outside his jurisdiction, sent word to the chancery. Arriving on the scene exactly one hour later, at 12 noon, the bishop of Antequera, Dominican Fray Juan Bartolomé de Bohórquez e Hinojosa, beheld the trunk's contents for himself. He declared the newly found face and hands to be a sign from heaven indicating that the Virgin should be Oaxaca's patroness and ordered that the statue of the Risen Christ be sent to the Hermitage of the Holy Cross.

Readers may already have noticed a strange emphasis on time in the foundational narrative. Indeed, devotion to the Virgin of Solitude displays an insistent, almost obsessive fascination with the measurement of human history. The most striking element—essential to any serious interpretation of her story—belongs to a much larger temporal framework. In what must surely be one of history's most uncanny feats of timing, Cortés and his men dropped anchor at the coast of what is now Veracruz on April 21, 1519, and set foot on Mexican soil April 22: Good Friday.

The presentation of sequence in the Soledad story becomes all the more intriguing once it is learned that the year of the discovery is under dispute. How can the precise times of day be known while the calendar year is not? Alternate dates place the event in 1617 or 1618, while a government plaque outside the basilica cites an even earlier date—1543! If this last year is accurate, the appearance of the image would have taken place barely fifteen years after the Dominicans arrived, in 1526, and only eleven years after a royal decree gave Antequera de Oaxaca the status of a city, in 1532.

One plausible explanation is that the Dominican bishop (dates of episcopate 1617–1633) legitimized an existing local devotion, formally recognizing both the propitious site and the miraculous image in order to provide a unifying symbol for the entire diocese.

Dates abound dizzyingly in the Soledad story, and the Virgin's faithful chronicler, Everardo Ramírez Bohórquez (remarkably, descended from the family of the bishop), delights in pointing out their coincidences. For instance, in 1697, the nuns who would attend the Virgin of Solitude arrived from Puebla at Oaxaca on January 14—the same date on which, in 1908, Oaxaca's archbishop received word that Pope Pius X had agreed to authorize the Virgin's coronation. Other coincidences were deliberate: in 1909, the crown was placed on her head ten minutes after 12 noon—the precise time of day, it is speculated, that the bishop of Antequera had declared her Oaxaca's patroness.[2]

For centuries, the eighteenth of each month has been designated in Oaxaca for veneration of the Virgin of Solitude. Different areas of the huge geographical expanse that formerly comprised the diocese of Antequera would take turns occupying the sanctuary in order to render her honor. And, whether by design or chance, in the ancient church a time-honored celebration of Mary's virginity took place each year on December 18.

The other aspect of the Soledad's foundational story which must surely have caught readers' attention is the fact that while *two* images were found, only one was immediately appointed Oaxaca's patron— but *not* the one representing the cornerstone of Christian theology!

An alternate version tells of *two* wooden chests, but whatever the number of trunks found in the discovery, reports agree that an intact, handsomely crafted statue of the Risen Christ was found along with Oaxaca's more celebrated religious artifact. The Second Person of the Trinity—the Incarnation of God portrayed in the glory of the Resurrection—was passed over for a mere set of hands and face as if this were the most obvious choice in the world.

The statue discovered along with the Virgin of Solitude can be found nowadays in the Church of Carmen Alto ("*alto*," "upper," signifies the social class of its colonial parishioners; indigenous, *mulatto*, and *mestizo* worshipers were relegated to the "lower" church of the same name). Christ's Mother reigns in a basilica as Oaxaca's queen while the Risen Christ lives in the side altar of a church that does not even bear his name. A small plaque tells of who he is to those curious enough to approach closely, but this identity has been largely eclipsed by the shadow of his beloved, prestigious Mother.

Depending on one's perspective, the choice of the one image over the other may be seen as heretical, ridiculous, or even comical. However, the preference of the *Mater Dolorosa* over the Risen Christ must be measured against the religious thought and practice of the time.

Laying historical ambiguity aside, both images arrived in Oaxaca bearing heavily suggestive symbolic associations. These had to be accommodated in a brand-new diocese being settled by Spanish Catholics struggling to establish themselves, while, simultaneously, indigenous populations, suffering under new forms of oppression and from previously-unknown diseases, were negotiating the positions they would take with regard to the imported religion of their conquerors. The religious images and the life situations of those who venerated them engaged in multivocal conversations. It was that dialogue that brought the delicate white face and hands "like lilies" to life.

✳ ✳ ✳ ✳ ✳

The valleys that now form the metropolitan area of Oaxaca's capital were inhabited by 10,000 BCE, and traces of the first villages date from the second millennium before the Common Era. Two rivers made of this area a fertile crescent at 1,500 meters above sea level. The temperate climate and flat expanses of land proved exceptionally amenable to cultivation.

A period of population growth occurred in the central valleys due to advances in agriculture, and archaeologists estimate that by around 500 BCE approximately 2,500 inhabitants lived in eighty communities. Urban centers arose, and a governing class controlled religion (including the calendar), war, communication, and resources. During the classical period, construction of the ceremonial center Monte Alban began. Towns and villages ringed the outskirts. A surge of growth took place and by 200 CE, the valleys' population reached approximately 14,500 inhabitants.

During the post-classic period, the Aztec Empire made inroads into Oaxaca, subjugating the Zapotec nation in 1486. Mexica conquerors set up a military post on a plain that, up until then, had been used primarily as the location for a huge regional market. The Mexica called this site "Huaxyacac," "place at the foot of the *huajes* (a tree that gives edible seeds)." This Nahuatl term displaced the natives' own names, "Luhulaa" and "Ñuhundua"—Zapotec and Mixtec, respectively—and was later hispanicized, evolving into the name that now designates both the state and its capital.

During his first conversations with Cortés, in answer to the insistent queries of the Spanish conquistador, Aztec emperor

Moctezuma told of gold in Tuxtepec (Oaxaca). In 1521, once Tenochtitlán had been secured, Cortés turned his sight southward. An expedition of thirty Spanish soldiers on horseback, another eighty on foot and four thousand indigenous allies took the central valleys. By 1522, "*La Segura de la Frontera*" ("the stronghold of the Frontier") was established, and by 1524, Huaxyacac was "pacified."

Cortés wanted this fertile valley all for his own, but incoming Spanish settlers had other ideas. They disregarded his orders—issued on three occasions—to withdraw from the lands of which they had taken possession, sending envoys to the Spanish Crown to argue their case. In 1526, a royal decree gave these inhabitants the right to settle "Antequera del Valle de Guaxaca." In 1529, the first mayor was appointed to govern the settlement's eighty Spanish families. Construction of streets and a plaza began. In 1532, Carlos V conferred on Antequera the status of a city, and in 1535, by papal bull Pope Paul III established Antequera as a diocese, one of the first in New Spain.

The Valley of Guaxaca (or "Guajaca") constituted an important link between South America and Central Mexico, since beyond Puebla travelers would find no other Spanish bastion until Guatemala (remember the mule caravan). The *city* of Oaxaca expanded rapidly because of its strategic location, coupled with the success of the silk trade in the Mixteca and Sierra Norte, the cochineal (dye) industry of the central valleys, and cotton production from the coast.

However, stabilizing the *state's* growth—especially in rural areas (where, even as late as 1800, 95 percent of Oaxaca's inhabitants lived)—would take much longer. The indigenous populations had been decimated by epidemics, and centuries would pass before they would reach their estimated pre-Conquest numbers.[3] Even up to the turn of the twentieth century, rural women commonly gave birth to six to ten or more children, only to see half of them die during childhood.

Although Pope Paul III had placed the diocese of Antequera under the protection of Mary of the Assumption, during colonial and post-colonial times the pallid, aristocratic figure of the Virgin of Solitude made a more fitting patroness. As if perceiving the triumph of the Assumption as premature, Oaxacans preferred their Virgin at the foot of the cross. Believers gravitated toward her image. During colonial times, her appeal extended beyond the state of Oaxaca: the borders of the diocese—which was much greater in territory than it is now—extended deep into Puebla, and the devotion claimed a strong following in Veracruz.

The Conquest—not an encounter (and even less a "discovery") but a violent, unequal clash between opposing civilizations—unequivocally set the context for the Soledad devotion in New Spain. Native, Spanish, and soon, *criollo* (Mexicans of Spanish descent), *mulatto* (mixed African, indigenous and/or Spanish), and *mestizo* (mixed indigenous and Spanish) Christians were obviously affected quite differently by the multiple problematics of this clash, but all experienced—in distinct forms and to different degrees—stress, hardships and suffering. This reality was symbolically expressed much more aptly by imagery of physical tribulations derived from Good Friday than by triumphal, ethereal symbolism drawn from the Resurrection.

The brutality of the crucifixion made explicit the very real and bloody nature of military domination. And the blood offering on the cross that procured salvation was comprehensible to the diverse indigenous nations, all of whom practiced to different degrees some form of bloodletting (of which human sacrifice was the most extreme) as a time-honored ritual technique of healing, propitiation, and renewal.[4]

Visitors to Latin American churches are often struck by the churches' gory portrayals of bleeding saints, virgins, and saviors in agony. And the most introductory lesson for pastoral workers accompanying Latin American faith communities is the precedence of Good Friday over Easter Sunday in popular celebrations. Spanish and Portuguese influences—at the time of the Conquest, dominated by this type of religious expression—took root in indigenous and African sensibilities, coinciding with the spiritual needs of these historically oppressed groups.

By the end of the seventeenth century, then, the Virgin of Solitude had become beloved by the people of Oaxaca and its neighboring states. The isolation felt by inhabitants of Mexico's southern states found expression in her solitude. Pilgrims endured an arduous journey to arrive at the impressive sanctuary with its huge atrium on the outskirts of an increasingly bustling, prosperous capital. A variety of traditional dances from various regions were enacted there in her honor, performed to exuberant musical accompaniment.[5]

As in the cases of the Virgin of Juquila and the Virgin of Guadalupe, devotion to the Virgin of Solitude conflated successfully with pre-existing indigenous traditions. The site on which the hermitage of St. Sebastian had been built was a "substitution shrine" for a native holy place known for its miraculous rock from which salt water flowed.

But unlike our other two virgins, this devotion has enjoyed uncontested, remarkable civil and ecclesial acceptance since its inception—in keeping with its foundational story, in which Bishop Bohórquez unhesitatingly sanctioned the discovered image. When construction of the church was undertaken in 1682, both canonical and royal permission had been sought and procured and the support of the viceroy obtained. A local dignitary reputed to be rich but parsimonious was convinced to adopt the project.

Acceptance came from the general public, as well. Fr. Fernando Méndez, the church's first rector, went door to door to collect funds. (According to legend, the first donation came in the form of jewelry from a wealthy woman with a checkered past—who from then on led an exemplary life.) The work was finished in 1689, and the church was consecrated in 1690.

The rock from which water seeped—and where the mysterious trunk of the mule train had been opened—was incorporated into the

The "weeping rock" where pilgrims offer coins and written notes

Colonial-era portrait of one of the first "Monicas"

sanctuary's architecture. The Virgin's "tears" were said to emanate from the church's stone pores.

As was customary, religious sisters were sought to tend to the image and sanctuary. From the beginning, Fr. Méndez had envisioned that the complex would include a convent. Groundwork for this was initiated at the same time that the church construction began, although the convent was not completed until 1697. The diocese petitioned for assignment of the cloistered Augustian nuns, *Religiosas Agustinas Recolectas de Santa Monica*, founded in Puebla under the town's eleventh bishop (whose heart is buried in the altar of the basilica in return for having sent his "Monicas" to Oaxaca). Reverend

Mother Teresa de Santa Cruz, Mother Ana de San José, Mother María de San José Tornera, Mother Antonia de la Madre de Dios, and Sister Teresa de San Miguel (at the time still a novice) took up residence in the convent, becoming acquainted with the image for whose care they had been contracted.

Not long after the Monicas' arrival, an incident took place that might have had dire consequences. Because of frequent exposure to candle smoke and incense—used especially by indigenous devotees—the Virgin's face and hands had been darkened. The sisters determined to wash them, and asked for wine that they intended to use for that purpose. Fr. Méndez cautioned that wine might damage the varnish, and the sisters decided to use only water and a bit of soap. Having done so, they returned the Virgin to her place. However, when the faithful encountered the white-faced Virgin in the temple, cries burst out in alarm, "You are not the Virgin of Solitude!"[6] Public outrage ensued. Oaxacans claimed that the Monicas had "cut off" the Virgin's head to send to their bishop in Puebla. At one point, a mob even threatened to drag the sisters from the convent. The city council and religious authorities had to intervene to quell the unrest.

The building that served as the convent, along with the entire complex, deserves admiration for its colonial-style beauty. But the basilica building itself is a triumph of architectural ambition. José Antonio Gay wrote of the Soledad that "its daring arches, haughty ceilings, and finesse of details equal the grandeur of intention which is manifested in their composition."[7] Sculpted in yellow stone overlaying the green *cantera*, the seventy-nine-foot high baroque façade was redone in 1717 and 1718 with twelve saints' statues set into the stonework. The façade's shape suggests the form of a huge *retablo* (altar piece). Constructed in traditional style, the building was designed as a cruciform. A monumental eight-foot organ, its original case dating from 1686 and its interior components from the eighteenth century, adds a note of cultured sophistication.

The main attraction, of course, has always been the Virgin herself. The delicate face and hands were ingeniously incorporated into the fashioning of a life-sized form, thus creating the appearance of a complete statue. Great pains are taken to ensure that these are the only elements of her body to show through the adorned robes. The tender face is strictly bordered from forehead to chin, and the fragile hands with no wrists peek out from underneath multiple layers of fabric. The pallor of her countenance and the details of her array follow the prescribed pattern of a manifestation of Mary beloved to Spanish Catholics, the *Mater Dolorosa*.

For while the *site* of the basilica remains perpetually indebted to its indigenous antecedents, where unquestionably the weeping rock played a formative role even until present times, the Virgin of Solitude is essentially a Spanish figure—albeit one with the potential to resonate deeply with the unarticulated sufferings of the native population.

European devotion to this presentation of the Virgin Mary bears a fascinating history of its own, a history that has fortunately been well researched by historians and theologians.[8] What I find most relevant for our purposes here is the way in which devotion to the Virgin of Solitude on both continents exemplifies on a small scale the wider-encompassing motif, that of the *Mater Dolorosa*. In Europe, devotion to the *Mater Dolorosa* arose as a string of local, popular practices for precisely the same reason that later ensured its longevity in Mexico, namely, that the motif "spoke to" the shared human experiences of believers. Devotional expressions multiplied to the extent that they migrated, spreading to other parts of continental Europe and the Americas, and eventually becoming encoded in the official universal liturgy.

Marian devotion intensified throughout Europe in the eleventh and twelfth centuries, and the *Mater Dolorosa*—as an object of devotion to the Virgin in her role as mother of the crucified Christ—seems to have appeared first toward the end of the eleventh century. Beginning in Northern Germany, Scandinavia, and Scotland, the motif later reached Italy and Spain, where it took firm root and dramatically proliferated from the mid-fourteenth century onward. Scholars attribute this to the timing at which the Black Death reached its height, around 1350. The first record of a local church celebrating a liturgy in honor of the sorrowful Virgin dates from April 22, 1423, in Cologne.

The *Mater Dolorosa* evolved more from a matrix than from a single devotion. It was a composite of symbolic representations, all of which found their ultimate significance in the cross. Developing trends in piety gave rise to titles such as "The Virgin of Sorrows" and "The Virgin of Solitude," or to such terms as "The Lamentations of

Mary" and "The Seven Sorrows" (drawn from biblical sources embellished by traditional retellings.[9]) The scriptures do not describe the Way of the Cross to the extent of detail with which Christians are familiar; its complexity is derived, rather, from tradition, which often cast Mary in a prominent role. In one scene, the Virgin Mary holds her Son's crucified body in what is now known as "The Deposition." This act is not explicitly mentioned in the Bible but was elaborated over the course of time in the Christian imagination, evolving into the posture of the Pietà. As if supplementing a male Passion with a female presence, devotional practices were improvised in which believers focused on the person of Mary in order to enter more experientially into Christ's death. Complementarity is not new to Mariology,[10] but these practices were, and religious sentiment of the time found expression in popular devotions to the *Mater Dolorosa*. The Friday before Good Friday became known as "Sorrowful Friday," devoted to the Virgin's witness of her son's Passion. The *Via Matris* (the Way of the Mother), usually held on Holy Saturday, traces backwards the Stations of the Cross—this time reenacting Mary's steps. The *Pésame* service, held on the evening of Good Friday (when, in tradition, Mary receives the broken body of Jesus from the cross), allows the faithful to give their condolences to Jesus' mother at his wake.

Of the many devotions that were developed during the Middle Ages, such as the Christmas crèche by the Franciscans or the rosary by the Dominicans, what I find most striking is that these diverse practices all intended to place believers "at the scene" of gospel events. Racked by heresies, wars, and the plague (which wiped out a fifth of Europe's population), local churches recognized in the *Mater Dolorosa*'s sorrowful face an expression of their own passion. On a spiritual level, these developing devotions impressed upon believers the importance of accompanying the Mother of God in her role as disciple of her son. The Virgin Mary had stood at the foot of Jesus' cross; Christians could best come close to him in his Passion by imitating her.

The enormously popular *Stabat Mater Dolorosa*, "The Sorrowful Mother Standing," a Latin poem translated into various European languages and set to music by a host of composers, exemplifies both this emphasis and its vast appeal. In singing the hymn, believers ask to join the Virgin's faithful, lonely vigil at the foot of the cross.

Much like the two images found mysteriously in a wooden trunk in Oaxaca, the *Stabat Mater* is one of two mirror poems—only one of which gained public acclaim. The mournful *Stabat Mater Dolorosa* and the exuberant *Stabat Mater Speciosa*, "The Joyful Mother Standing," follow the same literary pattern, but the *Speciosa*—a rhapsody in which Mary rejoices at Christ's birth—fell into almost complete oblivion until transcribed from a fifteenth-century manuscript in Paris in 1852. On the other hand, by the end of the fourteenth century, European Catholics of virtually all classes, nationalities, and backgrounds knew the *Stabat Mater Dolorosa*—even though it was not formally admitted to the liturgical prayer of the church until 1727.[11] (The *Stabat Mater* would eventually travel throughout the world; a contemporary collector I came across owns 212 versions in 21 languages.)

Visual art provided another way of expressing the intense popular piety centered on the *Mater Dolorosa*. The best European artists of their day portrayed in their paintings the Virgin's despair, anguish, and courage. In one of my favorite works, an early example produced by the fifteenth-century artist Dirk Bouts from the Netherlands, we see a white-faced, spent Madonna with silent tears and folded hands. During the following three centuries numerous artists would continue to render their own interpretations of ultimate suffering.

But originally, religious art depicted the *Mater Dolorosa* through statues. Especially in Spain, the *Mater Dolorosa* became popular in this medium beginning in the late sixteenth century. Light-weight, life-sized images fashioned in this unmistakable motif could be easily transported in processions, sighted readily by crowds who were thus encouraged to identify with the *Mater Dolorosa* as a human person.

Like the Immaculate Conception, the *Mater Dolorosa* in Europe eventually became a particularly *Spanish* devotion—for example, as Queen Isabella's favorite depiction of Mary. Spanish settlers brought representations of the sorrowful Virgin with them when they migrated to New Spain, not only to Oaxaca but to multiple colonial centers in Latin America. These images of the *Mater Dolorosa*, crafted in the Spanish motherland and known by different names (*Dolores, Soledad*, the related *Piedad*), became embedded in the devotional lives of colonial Mexico. In Querétaro even today thousands of devotees from all over the state walk in a nocturnal procession during Holy Week to reach their patroness's sanctuary. Customs such as this one recall the devotion's arrival to these lands, when the Virgin Mary's familiar, maternal presence, like a guiding star in the night sky, comforted settlers far from home.

❋   ❋   ❋   ❋   ❋

The roots of the Virgin Mary's role as guide to sailors are obscure in Europe. Scholars piecing together the origins of this phenomenon refer to a copyist's mistake, which substituted "*stella maris*," "star of the sea," for "*stilla maris*," "drop of the sea"—a suggested etymological root for Mary's Hebrew name, Miriam. Marina Warner writes, "The sway of astronomy over the medieval imagination was so strong, and the Virgin so closely identified with the heavens, that the slip of a scribe's hand introduced into Marian literature and art one of its most beautiful and suggestive metaphors."[12]

The mariners' hymn "*Ave Maris Stella,*" of unknown authorship, dates at least to the ninth century. Devotional practices such as this one grew in popularity among sailors during the centuries preceding the Conquest. Another Marian expert, historian Linda Hall, writes that Spanish mariners often sang the *Ave Maris Stella* at sundown for protection against the perils of the night and to welcome the Virgin's star, Polaris, essential to navigation. The *Stella Maris* merged not only with Polaris but also with the *Stella Matutina*, the Morning Star: the first star of the evening, the last star of the morning—the mariner's most constant companion during his loneliest hours.

In Oaxaca's coastal town of Puerto Escondido, every year a float bearing an adorned statue of the Virgin of Solitude is taken to the shore. The high point of the ceremony comes when the Virgin is carefully set into a fishing boat and taken for a brief excursion on the water. Amidst flowers and candles set floating on the ocean, this gesture asks a blessing for fishermen and others who make their living from the sea.

A friend who was born and raised in the capital recalls how, as a child, she loved going to the church on the Virgin's feast day to see the sailors from Veracruz process into the basilica, dressed in their white outfits accented with red scarves and performing the traditional foot-stomping for which their state is known. The dancing sailors had inherited the *Stella Maris* tradition, a remnant of Mexican colonial piety embodied in the figure of Oaxaca's most famous *Mater Dolorosa*. Women played a key role in this decidedly male custom: as the mother of Jesus kept vigil for her Son, now they waited for their men who spent long periods of time away from home.

Like her son who calmed tempestuous waters, the Virgin of Solitude was credited with the saving of many lives. It used to be said that sometimes during storms, sailors spotted her black-clad figure from the decks of their ships. Periodically, rumors circulated that upon opening the church in the morning, sacristans found the hem of the Virgin's robes damp with seawater. The miraculous rock at the basilica entrance no longer seeps water, but it is said that the roaring of the sea can be heard if one puts one's ear to the stone's surface.

During Lent in Oaxaca, the Virgin of Solitude's delicate hands, joined in prayer, are ringed with a crown of thorns. The three nails of the crucifixion are affixed so as to radiate over her chest. A sad mystery rests in the figure of her tired body and white face. This is no longer a triumphal Virgin. She is not young and fresh, but drawn and brooding. Her majestic trappings have been stripped away, and the darkness of her luxuriant velvet robe deepens and becomes as black as a starless night. She is in mourning.

In many parts of Latin America, the Friday of the week preceding Good Friday is still known as the "*Viernes de Dolores*," "Sorrowful Friday." The practice of setting up *altares de Dolores*—altars in homes and churches in honor of the Virgin of Sorrows—began in fifteenth-century Spain, and when this custom migrated with colonizers, it became inculturated as a particularly Mexican tradition. On the altar in the basilica are placed citrus fruits to represent bitterness; purple candles and flowers for the Passion; white flowers, customary for the dead; and water to symbolize the Virgin's weeping. Quick-growing seeds, such as barley or onion, are sown in the clay backs of animal figurines and represent the new life that will flower from the paschal event. Also typically displayed are allusions to the Passion, such as nails or a crown of thorns like those held by the hands of the Virgin. A tradition frequently practiced in the past (although nowadays not as common) was to distribute water—usually, flavored drinks—to visitors and passersby in commemoration of the Virgin's freely given tears.[13]

During Holy Week—especially the three days for which the statue is lowered from her golden footstool—the Soledad Basilica receives visitors from near and far. Pilgrims join local devotees who come from the neighborhood that bears her name or from other precincts of the capital to pay their respects.

Holy Week in Mexico is vacation season, and the Virgin draws tourists to view Oaxaca's pageantry. Gioacchino Rossini's *"Stabat Mater"* and a setting of the same by indigenous Oaxacan Juan Matías de los Reyes are played by the state's philharmonic orchestra. According to custom, on Good Friday evening, the archbishop himself delivers the *Pésame* sermon. A procession follows in which a replica of the image (the original figure is considered too fragile to be removed) is carried through the atrium downtown to the cathedral. The procession pauses to allow the Virgin to "meet" her son along the Way of the Cross (*"el Encuentro,"* "the Meeting").

Oaxaca is rightly celebrated for its richness of tradition. But the practice that stopped me in my tracks and took my breath away came from a simpler, less orchestrated expression of piety. One year, on the first day the Virgin spent lowered to the floor of the church, I joined the devotees who had gathered near her figure. As a crowd milled about the basilica—suddenly made all the more huge and echoing by the absence of the pews that had been removed in preparation for this practice—those nearest to the image knelt at the guardrail. A woman's soprano voice rose up as if from nowhere, in a melody that by turns soared, dipped, and rose. It reverberated so resoundingly through the basilica that, at first, I thought the song came from a sound system. Then I realized the melody came from a middle-aged woman kneeling at the guardrail. The solitary dirge fit perfectly the timbre of the Basilica and hit exactly the somber tone of the crowd gathered around the candle-lit image. As the voice continued at some length, shuddering in concentration and drenched in melancholy, I realized that she was singing the *Stabat Mater*:

At the cross her station keeping,
Stood the mournful Mother weeping,
Close to Jesus to the last.

Through her heart, His sorrow sharing,
All His bitter anguish bearing,
Now at length the sword had passed.

Oh, how sad and sore distressed
Was that Mother highly blest
Of the sole-begotten One!

Christ above in torment hangs;
She beneath beholds the pangs
Of her dying glorious Son.

Is there one who would not weep,
Overwhelmed by miseries so deep
Christ's dear Mother to behold?

Bruised, derided, cursed, defiled,
She beheld her tender child
All with bloody scourges rent.

For the sins of His own nation,
Saw Him hang in desolation,
Till His spirit forth He sent.

O thou Mother! Fount of love!
Touch my spirit from above;
Make my heart with thine accord.

Make me feel as thou hast felt;
Make my soul to glow and melt
With the love of Christ our Lord.

Holy Mother! Pierce me through;
In my heart each wound renew
Of my Savior crucified.

Let me share with thee His pain,
Who for all my sins was slain,
Who for me in torments died.

Let me mingle tears with thee,
Mourning Him who mourned for me,
All the days that I may live.

By the cross with thee to stay,
There with thee to weep and pray,
Is all I ask of thee to give.

Virgin of all virgins best,
Listen to my fond request
Let me share thy grief divine.

Let me, to my latest breath,
In my body bear the death
Of that dying Son of thine.

Wounded with His every wound,
Steep my soul till it hath swooned
In His very blood away.

Be to me, O Virgin, nigh,
Lest in flames I burn and die,
In His awful Judgment day.

Christ, when Thou shall call me hence,
Be Thy Mother my defense,
Be Thy cross my victory.

While my body here decays,
May my soul Thy goodness praise,
Safe in Paradise with Thee. Amen.[14]

It was as if this anonymous woman were singing for all of us. Her haunting voice sang of blood spilled over the centuries in a crucifixion that began on the Good Friday when conquistadors landed on American soil and continues into the present. And yet, more than a lament, it was a love song as well, offered in solidarity, meant to console the Virgin who accompanies her children in our times of trial and trouble. Now, we had come to grieve with *her*. Subconsciously melding our own sorrows, we merged them with hers in this regular, seasonal catharsis.

By standing in lonely vigil with the Virgin of Solitude—in the words of the *Stabat Mater*—devotees "feel her pain, so as to weep with her." If her suffering were not so compelling, we would not come. Even her silence pulses with the unspoken words, "His flesh, my flesh, his blood, my blood . . ."

She is silent, but she sees; she takes into her heart the fact of his death, even as she took into her heart the joy of his birth. Wishing she could die with him, wishing even more that she could die *for* him, all she can do is stand and watch—the last luxury of the oppressed. The refusal to close one's eyes to injustice: a bitter, remaining privilege, to stand in unrelenting vigil, faithful to the end.

Believers come because if we did not, we would miss the challenge of her witness—for that is what she does, give witness, standing perpetually at the foot of a cross throughout history. It is not that she accepts a murder carried out by a brutal empire in collusion with local rulers and the religious elite. It is that she accepts *being there.* She accepts the dare to simply stand there and *be alive* as the one she loves is about to die. It is her *Fiat* again, and again, her refusing to give up while not knowing how this unjust, unbearable death can ever be comprehended. It is embedding once more in human history her timeless surrender to Mystery, standing at the portal between life and death.

Her suffering evokes a response; her silence elicits this song. Almost too great to bear, her sorrow bends but does not break her. We have come to deliver our condolences: our *pésame.* She needs us.

✳   ✳   ✳   ✳   ✳

Saint Luke (in tradition, the first icon painter) describes Mary of Nazareth's capacity for reflection, for "pondering all these things in her heart" (2:51b), in an artful portrayal that has inspired generations of contemplatives and mystics throughout the centuries. Nowhere does her silence resound more than at the foot of the cross.

This quiet stance becomes all the more significant when one realizes that in many instances in the gospels, Mary the Mother of Jesus finds her voice.

St. Mark's overall portrayal of Mary may seem ambiguous and St. Matthew's birth narrative emphasizes the role of Joseph over that of Mary (who, in this text, is, indeed silent). But, from the first, in St. Luke's gospel Mary speaks—boldly, evocatively. Her words at the Annunciation rightfully hold a privileged place in Christian memory.

And in St. John's gospel, the Mother of Jesus exercises few—but key—roles in his ministry. In the first instance, at the wedding in Cana, she uses words judiciously and wisely. This passage is commonly regarded as the scriptural basis for Mary's role as intercessor. The second, considered the foundation for her identity as Mother of the church, takes place at the foot of the cross in a profound act of deep listening. The composite picture that emerges depicts a woman who knows the value of both speech and silence.

In every text where the evangelists allow her to speak, Mary of Nazareth defies the traditional stereotype that has muffled her voice through the ages. When Jesus does not join the group on the return trip of their pilgrimage and stays behind in Jerusalem, she calls her young son to task. She speaks out when she fears for his life because of the risks brought about by his ministry. She urges him to perform his first miracle—and thus plays a role in initiating his public life. She instructs others to trust and obey him, speaking as his first follower when even his disciples have yet to believe in him.

In a central place there is the Annunciation—the foundational text on which pivots Mary's holiness—telling a story *exactly opposite* to the one with which I was raised. For far from silent passivity, Mary's unsolicited verbal acceptance makes a definitive break with the literary genre of annunciations.[15] Her *Fiat*, freely and courageously articulated, ends forever the mute acquiescence of human history. The Annunciation story gives stunning evidence that God summons us to collaborate in salvation—and that we are expected to voice an answer.

How, then, can we understand Mary's silence at the foot of the cross?

Liberation theologian Jon Sobrino wrote that the world's poor need a love that is *effective*, that is, capable of transforming the miseries of the human condition, but they also look for a love that is *credible*.[16] Images such as the Virgin of Solitude are beloved because they give convincing expression to spiritual truths. The quiet stance of the Virgin at the foot of the cross makes her presence credible. At times, silence is the only appropriate response to acts of atrocity. Speech would trivialize the numinous awful reality, as if it could be reduced to words. Jesus' unjust and inhumane torture and execution are carried out in his mother's presence. In that moment, there is nothing but silence.

She is quiet; we must sing.

After hearing those winged words rise to the roof of the basilica, I realized the immense power of the *Mater Dolorosa*: She unleashes our voices. While giving us a repertoire with which to improvise, the Virgin of Solitude asks *us* to articulate who she is—who she is for us and who she is now. Like the medieval painters who tried their hand at portraying the *Mater Dolorosa*, or the millions who deliver their condolences at Good Friday's *Pésame* paraliturgy, or the single anonymous voice singing in the basilica, contemporary believers are urged by the compelling character of her image to portray her relevance for their own lives. She is silent *in order that we may learn to speak*. Like a good mother, she nurtures us to adulthood. She elicits a response. She safeguards our capability for expressing our own spiritual realities.

Opening ourselves to her suffering, we cleanse our own wounds as if with salt water. Like any therapy, it burns in the moment but leaves us whole, renewed. It opens new channels of empathy and compassion for our world, charting our course. Like a star affixed in the heavens, she remains for all time at her solitary post. A constellation, she shines from a heavenly throne, lighting the way.

For while the Virgin Mary in her manifestation as the *Mater Dolorosa* allows devotees a seasonal, communal catharsis, the Mother of God in the gospels acts primarily as a signifier, orienting fellow disciples toward her Son.

Two thousand years ago, a huddle of women watched just outside the city walls of Jerusalem as an insurgent, a heretic, a blasphemer, a revolutionary was nailed to a cross. These same women went to the tomb, overcoming their profound grief in order to witness for the beloved community where the broken body of the Messiah had been laid. They are the memory of the gospel, the subversive refusal to forget. While evangelists' versions vary, all place the faithful women—including Mary—in the definitive episode of Christ's revelation. They will be entrusted with the good news of the Resurrection. In their female company, the Virgin Mary tastes the deepest suffering and the sweetest joy.

✳ ✳ ✳ ✳ ✳

The story of Christianity tells of a marginal Jew who triumphed in glory, of a village woman who was crowned in heaven. Our interest here is to explore how in Oaxaca the Virgin of Soledad—mother of history's most famous victim—seems to always end up on the winning side.

A first example concerns the role of *Mater Dolorosa* in Mexico as a whole. At the patronal feast of Dolores on the evening of September 15, in the state that now bears his name, a Mexican-born priest of Spanish descent issued the famous "*Grito de Dolores*," "Cry of Dolores." When the plans of Fr. Miguel Hidalgo Costilla and his circle of conspirators (who had been waiting to launch an armed campaign) were discovered, Hidalgo precipitated the battle for Mexican independence on the Virgin's feast.

The second relates specifically to our Oaxacan *Mater Dolorosa*. After Hidalgo's arrest, another *criollo* priest, Fr. Jose María Morelos Pavón, took his place. Unlike the priests, who largely supported the independence movement (many even took up arms and joined its ranks), most Mexican bishops remained faithful to the crown. In Oaxaca, battalions of loyalist troops were recruited and enlisted by the Catholic Church! But when Morelos and his forces entered the city of Oaxaca in 1812, he declared the Virgin of Solitude the "*Capitana de la Insurgencia*," "Captain of the Insurgency."

The Soledad Basilica at dusk

Morelos's designation did not catch on in the rest of the country. The Virgin of Guadalupe continued in this role, but the incident does reveal that the Virgin of Solitude inspired followers on both sides of the struggle for independence. Although their superiors would defrock them before their execution by firing squad, these two priests found in the sorrowful Virgin's symbol an authentic religious symbol for their cause. Once independence was achieved, she emerged, victorious, with the *criollos*.

Several decades later, just down the street from the Soledad sanctuary, a Zapotec lawyer married a young woman from one of the capital's leading families. Benito Juárez, an orphan who as a child had tended his uncle's sheep in the Sierra Norte, was elected to lead Oaxaca in 1847. (He would subsequently be elected president of the Republic—the first indigenous president in the Americas.) As governor, he introduced the telegraph, an innovation that eased Oaxaca's isolation from the rest of the country, and implemented urban planning for the compact city that was already expanding beyond its river boundaries.

Juárez left a lasting national legacy by drafting Mexico's constitution, including the 1856 *Leyes de Reforma*, Laws of Reform, which limited the role of religion in public affairs. Ex-clausturation laws justified the confiscation of church property, allowing seizure of the Soledad convent property by municipal authorities. The religious orders entrusted with care of the Soledad's famous virgin (of whom the Monicas had been the first) were evicted. Today, the building houses the government offices of the capital city.

Across the street from the Soledad church, within view from its *cantera* steps, another infamous future president was born. A military general, Porfirio Díaz rose to power with his 1866 defeat of the French forces that had overtaken Mexico (and had occupied Oaxaca since 1864). His presidency—which turned into a dictatorship—coincided with a period of population growth during which, for the first time since the Conquest, Mexico annually registered more births than deaths.

Díaz believed in modernization and progress, and kept a daily pulse on the happenings in his home state through an extensive network of personal and political contacts. As a result, along with other urban areas, the city of Oaxaca prospered during the tenure of the dictator. By 1892, a railway connected Oaxaca with central Mexico.

Ports like Salina Cruz (opened in 1907) provided another means of transportation.

Now in communication with the rest of the Republic—and with Mexican national politics dominated for fifty years by two of its own—at the turn of the century, it looked as if Oaxaca's isolation belonged to the past. The *soledad* (solitude) that the capital had shared with its patroness, it was assumed, would melt into oblivion.

*   *   *   *   *

Behind the basilica building, tucked away in the least-frequented area of the complex, visitors can spend time in a small museum devoted entirely to the Virgin of Solitude. It opens at 10 AM, or anytime afterward when the attendant has finished mopping the entryway. A donation is solicited (she says off-handedly, "a coin, any coin you like"). Each time I visited the museum, I had its three dusty rooms to myself. With a million questions and no one to answer them, I wandered in silence, taking in displays of artifacts such as those found in my grandmother's attic. Large, dark religious paintings in poor condition. A pepto-bismol-pink porcelain tea service. A grandfather clock that had stopped counting time at 9:45. An ancient silver sword engraved with the Virgin's name. Dusty velvet swaths on which rest pieces of antique jewelry—such as a pair of tarnished wedding rings accompanied by a scripted note too faded to read.

In their gratitude, devotees over the centuries have offered objects of sentimental and monetary value as testimony to the Virgin of Solitude's relevance to their lives. Many of the names of donors belong to Oaxaca's leading capital families. Other tokens of gratitude remind viewers of her marine constituency: miniature wooden ships with intricate rigging, creations of seashells glued together, pearls nestled in open oyster shells. And then there are the *ex-votos*—whole walls of them—small paintings that tell of favors received. Several have to do with miracles at sea. Most illustrate the Virgin's intervention in cases of sickness, accidents, and miscellaneous misfortunes.

Ancient-looking paper money, no longer in circulation, from Nicaragua, Cuba, the United States, Canada, Brazil, Venezuela, Turkey, and Germany testifies to the far-reaching horizons of the Virgin's devotees.

A view of the facade of the Soledad Basilica

Glass cases exhibit her faded costumes of past ages, her worn, trademark black robes still glistening with gold brocade. Vestments and other artifacts from previous rectors are set beside the Virgin's obsolete robes for display. In a black-and-white photograph Oaxaca's first archbishop looks back at viewers. The picture is surrounded by other items that at one time belonged to this influential devotee of the Virgin.

In the hallway, a series of four no-longer-in-use stained-glass representations (corrupted irreparably into shards in one corner) tells the story of the fateful day when the Virgin sealed her fate forever with that of the people of Oaxaca. In one panel, the enigmatic mule lies down on the famous rock and expires with her last breath.

The museum is populated by a host of ghostly religious figures. Exquisitely dressed statues of the child Jesus, *el Niño Dios*, are set up for display. In one, a toddler wearing a beige robe, floral circlet atop his golden tresses and eyelashes curling over his cheek, sits in a chair while attractively arranged *milagritos* swirl behind him on a red velvet background. Other statues and paintings depict a more sobering piety, in which the motif of the *Mater Dolorosa* dominates. A life-sized crucified Christ bleeds in a gilded glass coffin. Exaggerated expressions of outdated taste—many of dubious artistic quality—give an overall impression of dark anachronism.

For the Virgin of Soledad has seen better days. In recent years, her vitality has waned, both for seafaring pilgrims from Veracruz and for her subjects in Oaxaca. I do not mean to suggest that the devotion does not still exercise influence. She is, after all (as the gold lettering on her chamber reminds us), Queen of Oaxaca and patroness of the Archdiocese of Antequera. "Soledad" is a popular name, and numerous Oaxacan businesses bear her title. The centennial of the coronation in January 2009 provided the setting for a resurgence of fervor. But, compared to her immense appeal in the past—when devotees regularly streamed into the sanctuary to engulf her statue—the present state of the Soledad devotion leaves the Virgin standing lonely, a solitary beacon. Everardo Ramírez Bohórquez, the Virgin's faithful contemporary chronicler, recalls that on the eighteenth of each month, the visits of so many different pilgrimage groups required that mornings be allotted for outside groups and afternoons be designated for local ones. The Virgin's feast day convened one of the largest fairs of the Republic's southern states. Oaxacans "*de casa*," "from home"—in other words, of the capital area—expressed their devotion in the novena before the celebration, since on December 18 the sanctuary was overrun by pilgrims from outside its environs.

Nowadays, *veracruzanos* are more likely to set out for Juquila than the basilica. A local newspaper reported some 100,000 pilgrims at last year's Soledad festival—crowds far smaller than those that inundated the home of the state's *un*official patroness throughout that same month (even though visiting the less prestigious sanctuary entails a far more demanding trip).

When migrants go north, the Juquilita—herself a traveler—more adeptly crosses the border and, as Empress of the Americas, the Guadalupana outranks the Queen of Oaxaca. Unlike the Virgin of Guadalupe, the Spanish Soledad's image itself is not encoded with indigenous symbolism. Her foundational narrative does not cast a Juan Diego Cuauhtlatoatzin or a Chatino catequist in a major role. And, unlike Juquila—a Spanish statue left under indigenous charge for long enough that she "went native"—the Virgin of Soledad still has an aristocratic countenance: contrast the stories of the fire that permanently darkened the Juquilita's face with the nearly disastrous incident involving the Monicas, from which the Soledad image emerged with white face intact.

How could a symbol that vividly embodied Oaxacan *communitas* for almost four centuries fade in vitality? The decline of the small fishing industry provides a partial explanation for the decrease in devotees from Veracruz. But in the same state, a parallel phenomenon—namely, the drop in coffee prices that displaced hundreds of thousands of people in farming communities in recent years—drove *more*, not *fewer* pilgrims to Juquila.

The Virgin of Solitude's loss of popularity cannot be explained, either, by the simple fact that the territory over which she reigns has been reduced. Until 1962, Tehuacán, Puebla, had belonged to the archdiocese of Antequera, when it passed to the archdiocese of Puebla. In 1979, Tuxtepec was constituted as its own diocese. At one time, Puerto Escondido, Huajuapam de León, the Isthmus of Tehuantepec, and the various indigenous prelatures of the state all belonged to Antequera—one of the most prestigious dioceses in New Spain.

Borders, even ecclesial ones, need not limit the Virgin Mary. Besides, the sheer numbers of people living nearest her throne have multiplied exponentially during past decades.

No, the loss of ground must be explained in other terms.

My research has forced me to surmise that at a certain moment in time, the Virgin of Solitude—symbolizing, as she does, the collective unconscious of Oaxaca—became *too* closely identified with the church hierarchy and state government. This reinforced alliance set the trajectory that propelled the devotion through the last century but also toward a sad decline in the new millennium. Popular religious practice is deceptively conservative but stubbornly populist. Thoroughly traditional (even exaggeratedly orthodox) in appearance, it balks at being "used." Victor and Edith Turner observe that when those in hierarchical positions—whether these are commercial, ecclesial, or political—are perceived as habitually taking advantage of a symbol's power, its sanctuary's following falls off and, over time, detached devotees search for a more authentic pilgrimage site.

Shortly after the turn of the twentieth century, the Virgin of Solitude was crowned. A singular honor granted only to select representations of the Virgin Mary, this privilege was procured through a request for papal authorization submitted by the archdiocese. Basking
in the optimism of Oaxaca's growth under the tenure of Porfirio
Díaz, backed by the assent of the state government, clerics had sent a
petition for coronation to the Holy See. Preliminary news of papal approval arrived on January 14, 1908; the official communiqué from
Pope Pius X was announced on January 18. On May 12 (the day Oaxaca pays special tribute to the Virgin of Guadalupe), Monseñor Eulo-
gio Gillow issued an edict announcing a huge archdiocesan celebration for the coronation. By any standard, it was an ambitious
undertaking.

Preparations for the lavish ceremony cemented the prestige of the
local hierarchy and of capital and state politicians. Following Oaxaca's
succession of twenty-nine bishops, Monseñor Gillow had become the
first "*Arch*bishop of Antequera"; the coronation became the crown-
piece of his episcopate. As a member of Díaz's network of contacts,
Gillow achieved a truce between church and state and recovered con-
fiscated property. He had already negotiated the return of the magnificent church of Santo Domingo; now, he orchestrated what might
be considered Oaxaca's finest hour.

Restoration of the Soledad church was overseen by Gillow himself. The Virgin's chamber was redesigned. Stained-glass panels and
marble flooring were installed. A residence—designed in colonial style
and utilizing *cantera* stone—was constructed downtown specifically
to host the papal delegate and prelates of the Mexican hierarchy who
would attend the ceremony. The Virgin's crown was made in Paris,
set with precious gems (including emeralds and diamonds that had
belonged to Gillow's own mother). A church bell for the cathedral
was forged for the occasion, and it was rung for the first time during
the coronation. At ten minutes after 12 noon on January 18 in 1909,
the exquisite diadem was placed on the Virgin's head in an event of
unequaled distinction for Oaxaca.

Since the Soledad devotion so clearly represented *communitas* in
Oaxaca, readers may not be surprised to learn that the coronation coincided with another triumph: during this period—for the first time
since the Conquest—the state population passed the million mark.[17]

The day after the coronation, the Fourth National Catholic Congress opened in Oaxaca, hosted by Gillow (who gave the keynote presentation). Held in the complex of Santo Domingo Church, the Congress addressed the revolutionary fervor then sweeping the country. Expositions dealt with religious topics (the persistence of idolatry, religious education) and social issues (alcoholism, salaries and working conditions, problems faced by agricultural workers). The closing speech, given by a prominent lay Catholic intellectual and journalist, alluded to the coming of major changes. These would find expression the following year, in the 1910 Mexican Revolution.

For, while the Porfirian tenure had brought wealth to select areas of the country—Oaxaca City among them—it had also exacerbated the gap between rich and poor. On the eve of the Revolution, only 2.5 percent of the households in rural Mexico owned land. In Oaxaca, some two hundred haciendas existed in the state, some with land expanses of up to 30,000 hectares, the majority clustered in the vicinity of the capital.

The Oaxacan-born dictator had also stifled political liberty. The *Asociación Juárez,* "Juárez Association," was founded in 1901, but by 1906, one of its founders, the intellectual Ricardo Flores Magón, had had to flee to Canada as a political refugee. While their queen was crowned in an opulent ceremony, indigenous, *mulatto,* and *mestizo* populations lived in abject poverty. Gilded standards proclaimed her sovereignty, but an estimated nine out of ten Oaxacans could not read.

During the years immediately preceding the coronation, foreign investors bought major shares in Oaxacan land and industries at Diaz's invitation. Mining peaked at the turn of the twentieth century: an estimated 10 million U.S. dollars were invested in some 100 companies. Commercial agriculture in many areas replaced subsistence farming. The cultivation of coffee spread rapidly in the last quarter of the nineteenth century in the Sierra Norte, the Isthmus of Tehuantepec, and the area around Juquila. Local consumption of coffee began to displace the traditional drinking of hot chocolate. More important, government seizures of communal lands for privately held, foreign-owned coffee plantations sparked rebellions of a ferocious tenacity unseen since the Conquest.

The most violent incident occurred in Juquila.

When Chatino small farmers organized to repel outsiders who had expropriated their lands, Díaz struck mercilessly. In 1896, military troops were sent to Juquila to crush the uprising. A massacre took place in the sanctuary's church atrium, where blood stained its stone floor. Those Chatinos who were not killed outright died en route to Mexico City or were forced to join the federal army—a conscription that effectively meant exile.

In 1911, two years after the triumphal crowning of Oaxaca's queen, Gillow signed a pastoral letter calling for Oaxacans to resist the chaos of the Revolution that had overtaken Oaxaca. The ensuing decades swirled with commotion, during which the Virgin remained quietly on her throne as if immune to turmoil. In spite of damage to the church, the bejeweled Virgin emerged unharmed from the earthquakes of 1928 and 1931 (the altar and the Virgin's niche were re-done with gold overlay in 1933). In 1947, a spate of civil unrest overthrew Oaxaca's governor, briefly causing riots in the capital;[18] the stately Virgin continued standing, unscathed.

The city of Oaxaca eventually regained stability and enjoyed a period of relative peace and prosperity in the 1950s. As the Jubilee of the Virgin's coronation approached, a committee was formed to begin preparations for the commemoration. Headed by a society woman from one of the capital's leading families and composed of prominent citizens (the chronicler, Ramírez, among them), the committee's principal task consisted in envisioning how their celebration would compare to the grandiose ceremony of fifty years past. In 1909, through its queen's coronation, Oaxaca had proven itself as a first-class city and claimed its rightful place in the Catholic world. The jubilee celebration would take a different emphasis.

In a spirit of nativism, the committee decided to commission a new crown. Unlike the French creation, this one would be made with strictly Mexican contributions and crafted by Oaxacan hands. Enlisting the talent of a renowned local goldsmith, the committee centered preparations for the jubilee celebration on the manufacture of a diadem that would represent "a true material expression of all Oaxacans."[19] The campaign enjoyed enormous popular support. A public appeal made for contributions brought in gold, pearls, and other precious gems for the project. Radio marathons were held to reach the goal, keeping listeners abreast of the campaign's progress hour by hour. It seemed that every Oaxacan matron in the capital donated an item of jewelry; sailors from Veracruz supplied pearls.

While the campaign appealed to devotees of all social classes and backgrounds, the celebration reaffirmed the Virgin's alignment with church and civil authorities. Engraved in the gold of the new crown appeared six standards, each belonging to a different stage of the Soledad devotion: that of the city of Oaxaca, from 1532; that of Bohórquez, the Dominican archbishop who had received the image in 1620; that of the benefactor who financed construction at the end of the seventeenth century; that of Pope Pius X, who had authorized the coronation; that of Gillow; and that of the archbishop who presided at the time of the jubilee.

The newly named, first Mexican cardinal came from Guadalajara to attend the jubilee. Ramírez describes the event as a "great feast" for the Oaxacan people, who "once more demonstrated their unity in this act of reverence and love" toward their patroness, as well as for the sailors who "often bring her pearls from the exotic East."[20]

During preparations for the jubilee, a petition had been submitted to the Holy See that the sanctuary be elevated to the rank of basilica. This concession was granted by Pope John XXIII and officially implemented on January 18, 1960, when the archbishop celebrated Mass in the newly declared Minor Basilica of Our Lady of Solitude.

The walls of the Soledad church are cluttered with articles of history. Plaques inform visitors of various dates of importance, while the Virgin watches impassively (as if unimpressed with the temporal artifacts that her devotees take so seriously). Alongside the one commemorating the elevation of the church status, another Oaxacan triumph is announced: during his first trip to the Americas, John Paul II visited the Basilica of Our Lady of Solitude on January 29, 1979. In the atrium, a government plaque relates that in 1987, Oaxaca's historic downtown (which includes the basilica) was declared a "Patrimony of Humanity" by the United Nations Educational, Scientific and Cultural Organization.

Our story now takes a despicable turn. In an act that would cause the Oaxacan church chagrin for years to come, on the morning of January 10, 1991, sacristans discovered that the Virgin's crown, jeweled rosary, and lily had been stolen. A police investigation deduced that robbers had hidden in the choir loft the day before. Once darkness had fallen, they let themselves down with a rope. They broke the lock that protected the Virgin's niche and then made off with the three precious items that comprised the Soledad trademark.

On that day, Oaxaca lost its innocence.

Waves of shock and indignation reverberated throughout the state, neighboring Veracruz, and all of Mexico; at that time, stealing from a church was unheard of. (Tragically, in Oaxaca alone, during the three years my family lived there, more than twenty-five churches were robbed.)

While lamenting the loss of the rosary and the lily, it was the theft of the crown that most injured Oaxacans' sensibility. As a symbol of unity—even for non-Catholics who considered the Soledad devotion part and parcel of the state's artistic and cultural patrimony—the crown's value surpassed its material worth. As Ramírez wrote in sorrow and outrage, "Apart from the profanation, condemned on all sides, a gem of incalculable value has been lost to us, because in it was forged a tradition of love, preserved and made credible over three and a half centuries."[21] Weighing two kilograms of gold, set with some six hundred diamonds and an extravagance of pearls, the crown represented innumerable favors received through the Virgin's intercession and thousands of expressions of piety: the spiritual wealth of Oaxaca. Another committee was formed, this time to replace the Virgin's stolen jewels, but the resounding success of the jubilee preparations would never be repeated. A new crown was procured; however, no diadem could take the place of one fashioned from the spontaneous gratitude of a populace united in fervent devotion. A replacement lily made of white gold was donated by a prominent Oaxacan couple and a rosary by the next archbishop. But these were isolated acts of generosity in honor of Oaxaca's patroness, remnants of a devotion that was already losing step with the state's hectic pace.

Bereft of the crown that symbolized her subjects' fidelity, the Virgin presided wearily over the capital as it grew exponentially, inundated with internal migrants seeking to escape rural poverty. Shantytown neighborhoods were cropping up beyond the boundaries of the two rivers that used to hem the metropolitan area. The state population, too, increased dramatically: from 1960 (just after the jubilee and the elevation of the church's status to basilica) to 1990 (just before the infamous robbery), the number of Oaxaca's inhabitants almost doubled.[22]

The crown—never recovered—symbolizes a bygone era in which religious naiveté, ecclesial triumphalism, and a homogenous worldview reigned. It recalls a time before the capital's monstrous growth, as one woman reminisced, when each neighborhood's families knew each other and no one had to lock their doors.

Tensions ran high in the aftermath of the robbery. The loss of the crown deeply affected a population already experiencing the stress of Oaxaca's rapid growth and divisions within the church.

The archbishop at the time of the theft, Bartolomé Carrasco Briseño (dates of episcopate 1976 to 1993), influenced by Latin American liberation theology, had established pastoral changes in Antequera. Carrasco's innovations included formation programs for youth and lay leaders; the introduction of base ecclesial communities (faith-sharing groups that read the Bible through the lens of social justice); dialogue with indigenous Catholics on religion and native culture; support of human rights organizations; and a regional seminary with a reputation for progressive theology. The result was the rise of a whole generation of pastoral workers loyal to Carrasco—whom most referred to affectionately as "don Bartolomé"—marked by their dedication to solving Oaxaca's social problems and working alongside its poorest people.

Carrasco's defense of human rights and indigenous communities brought the archdiocese into frequent clashes with the state government. Their antagonistic relationship hit its lowest point at the time of the robbery.[23] In the aftermath of the theft, one priest told me, a riot broke out at a rally convened by church leaders. Infiltrators sent by the state government, he claimed, had incited the crowd to blame Carrasco for the loss of Oaxaca's treasured heirloom. This priest had to block don Bartolomé with his own body, whisking him away to safety in the basilica complex, to protect the archbishop's safety—much as the Monicas had to be shielded from a mob four centuries earlier.

Perhaps the reality of the state over which the Virgin presides was never so golden as it appears in hindsight. The state population was certainly never homogenous (as recently as 1930, fully a third of its inhabitants did not speak Spanish). Carrasco's church had come into conflict with the state government precisely because its pastoral emphasis exposed problems of poverty and social inequality that lay hidden under the capital's cosmopolitan surface. The theft of the crown, then, marked a turning point in the state's reality and also in its self-image—its *perception* of that reality.

The robbery and its aftermath made visible a rupture of the alliance between church and state that had so favored the devotion in the past. Indebted as it had been to this alliance, the Soledad tradition was weakened by its dilution, while, at the same time, its close association with the status quo in the past discouraged the Virgin's identification with the emerging popular church. During subsequent administrations, the generation formed under Carrasco continued its pastoral accompaniment of poor communities and defense of human rights, while Antequera's next archbishop attempted to stabilize the tenuous church/state relationship strained during Carrasco's episcopate.

Would the Virgin of Solitude be able to project an authentic, convincing expression of Oaxacan *communitas* into the future? I came to no definitive answer. The ceremonies commemorating the Soledad coronation brought Oaxacans together once more in unity at her feet during the month of January in 2009. At a culminating liturgy, the original statue itself was taken to the capital's Guelaguetza Stadium for a huge Mass. Will the commemoration be enough to revive popular fervor?

Equally mystifying to me was the timing that placed me at her feet: Oaxaca's underlying social problems erupted while my family lived there, and I often wondered at how—of all the moments when we might have landed in Oaxaca—our stay had happened to coincide with the conflict. Already familiar with her figure, I sought Soledad's calm presence in the Soledad Basilica often during those months of crisis.

*   *   *   *   *

In 2006, a stand-off between the state chapter of the teachers' union and the governor suddenly erupted. The population—especially in the capital—was held captive by fear of the violence that had taken so many lives. Activities of daily life (such as classes in public schools) were suspended. Like a pressure cooker whose lid had blown off, many sectors of society used the conflict to express their dissatisfaction with Oaxaca's political system, widely regarded as corrupt. The teachers and the popular movement took over the main plaza for seven months in a huge sit-in. Tourism, which accounts for 80 percent of the capital's income, ground to a halt.

Antequera's archbishop, who had only recently arrived in Oaxaca, called for a return to order, as Gillow had done during the Revolution. His attempts at neutrality, unfortunately, were viewed as lukewarm by both sides (graffiti on the green *cantera* stone of the cathedral demanded bluntly, "Clarify your position: are you with us, or against us?").[24]

At the same site in Oaxaca where almost a century earlier Mexican Catholics had anticipated the 1910 Revolution, Santo Domingo Church hosted an ecumenical gathering in support of the popular movement, with Carrasco's former colleague, San Cristobal's bishop emeritus Samuel Ruiz García, as keynote speaker. As the months dragged on, the economy—so dependent on tourism—plummeted while violent clashes between police and protestors escalated. Delinquency by vandals increased. The city (like many other parts of the state) was paralyzed while the state government tried to alternately intimidate and outlast the movement.

The Virgin Mary was enlisted by both sides. The archbishop proposed that Catholics recite the Angelus for peace. Others began to pray the Magnificat, traditionally used in Latin America for desperate causes. I heard of trips to Juquila or the Basilica of the Virgin of Guadalupe to

An effigy in downtown Oaxaca during the teachers' strike

ask for miraculous intercession. A small handful of devotees prayed regularly at the Basilica of Soledad. The rumor circulated that the *mancha*—the dark stain that appears on the Virgin of Solitude's face during
Oaxaca's times of trouble—was being sighted by believers.

But on the main plaza, the seat of the popular movement, the Virgin of Solitude was nowhere to be seen. Reflecting Mexico's characteristic juxtaposition of devotionalism and anti-clericalism, two Popular Assembly leaders told me as we conversed at the improvised shrine
on the plaza's kiosk that the Catholic Church did not support their
movement. Posters bearing photos of political prisoners were hung
nearby; fresh flowers were set out; a candle burned day and night.
The Virgin of Juquila and the Virgin of Guadalupe, together with a
cross on which a map of the state of Oaxaca was crucified, made ap-
pearances, but the patroness of Oaxaca was conspicuously absent. The
fact that the oversight was unintentional only highlighted the significance of the omission.

The popular movement's altar on the main plaza

The priest who had whisked Carrasco from the angry mob after the theft of the Virgin's crown spoke to me about the silence regarding Soledad in public discourse during those difficult months. Speaking about the conflict in general, he lamented the absence of the Virgin of Solitude: "She should have been there; as mother of all Oaxacans, she should have been present."

As the conflict stagnated, members of the Popular Assembly and the teachers' union set out on a nineteen-day march that showed all the markings of a pilgrimage. Walking to Mexico City through four states to petition for intercession by the Mexican Congress, they set up an encampment at the feet of Benito Juárez's statue.

The pacifist Mayan community, "*Las Abejas*," "The Honeybees" —brought to international attention when their members were massacred in Acteal, Chiapas—made a pilgrimage to Oaxaca to bring a message of solidarity and a plea for non-violence, which they read at their pilgrimage's destination, the Soledad Basilica, on November 9, 2006.

For by then the conflict had taken many lives.

The archbishop presided over the funeral of the first casualty,[25] a protestor shot and killed during a march on August 10. The coffin was passed over the heads of the crowd like the white crest of a wave over a sea of mourners.

On the early morning of August 21, church bells rang throughout the capital and central valleys as a "caravan of death," a convoy of vehicles of assassins, circled the city, opening fire on protestors guarding movement-held radio and TV stations. An architect who worked for the school system died later that morning. From then on, neighbors began to set up nightly barricades to block traffic. On October 18, as negotiations broke down yet again, with teachers now divided as to whether or not to return to classes, a Zapotec-speaking teacher originally from the Sierra Norte was killed in a drive-by shooting on his return from a union meeting.

Since the beginning of the stand-off, both sides had pleaded for federal intervention: the governor sought troops, while the popular movement—like the archdiocese and a third of its priests—petitioned that the military *not* be employed.

On one of those perfect Oaxacan days in late October when the sky, cleared by the seasonal rains that green the capital's valleys,

shimmers like a jewel, heli-
copters began circling overhead. The Federal Preven-
tative Police of the Mexican
Army—complete with ar-
mored cars, high-powered
assault weapons, and tear
gas—advanced on the met-
ropolitan area. One of the
main thoroughfares they
traveled was Independence
Street—home of the Basil-
ica of Soledad. Troops in
full riot gear marched underneath the gaze of the
replica of the Virgin set in
the basilica's outer walls.

While not all Oaxacans
supported the movement,
the occupation by federal
troops was universally perceived as an insufferable af-
front to state dignity. The
takeover by army troops

*A teacher walks in front of
military tanks on the main plaza*

prompted an outpouring of
communitas. Tires were burned all over the city to dim pilots' visibility.
Movement radio stations provided twenty-four-hour coverage describing the advance of the army—and listeners rushed out to block its path.
All over the metropolitan area, strategic points of entry were barricaded
by citizens trying to repel the troops.

In our neighborhood, men and women—youth, elderly people,
and even children—filled the streets. Putting hips and hands to work,
they tipped over a bus to block the road. Forming a human shield, the
crowd swelled to prevent the soldiers from crossing the bridge that
separates our town from the capital. For two hours, our neighbors
held the troops at bay. As the front line of resisters would fall back
into the crowd, overcome by exhaustion and tear gas, others moved
up to take their place. The army finally retreated and looked for another route.

Although our neighbors held the bridge, the soldiers, inevitably, took over the city. By Christmas, after a great deal of national and international pressure, the troops were recalled—and graffiti was painted over in time for the tourist season. But the injuries of those traumatic six months cannot be erased so easily. In an emotionally charged testimony, a graduate student in her late twenties told of how she was arrested and held prisoner for five months and five days. On November 25 she had gone to a march that had turned into an ugly confrontation between a minority group of protestors and police. The state government—buttressed by the army—used the violent reaction of one faction of the Popular Assembly as an excuse to crush the movement.

At the same demonstration, a middle-aged woman from one of Oaxaca's base ecclesial communities suffered two broken ribs and a permanently injured hand when arrested.[26] Both prisoners were denied contact with family, pastoral agents, or legal counsel; after spending the night in a local jail, they and 140 others (including three minors) were flown six states away to a medium-security prison. Once in flight over the ocean, the young woman reported, the soldiers taunted prisoners that they would throw them into the water below.[27]

As the conflict abated, the teachers' union split into two entities. The weakened Popular Assembly vowed to continue to address the state's economic disparity, racism against indigenous and Afro-mestizos, political corruption, and flagrant human rights abuses. Emigration increased, driven by the conflict's economic drain. Oaxacans all over the state still attempt to recover from financial losses and to stabilize local governments. The conflict subsided, but political violence has continued or even worsened. Crimes related to narco-trafficking have spiraled and spates of kidnapping for ransom—previously unheard of in Oaxaca—have become common.

Perhaps the climate of economic precariousness and generalized violence suits the Soledad devotion more than the episode of political activism during which her image—traditionally so tied to the status quo—receded into obscurity. A new consciousness about Oaxaca's reality seems to have taken root, but results remain to be seen. From her pedestal, the Virgin stands watching. Her replica, lit by a fluorescent lantern, overlooks the thoroughfare to the city's main plaza, like a beacon lighting the way.

✳ ✳ ✳ ✳ ✳

The story of the Virgin of Solitude raises obvious questions. Do popular faith expressions centered on the Virgin Mary offer a catharsis (the "opiate of the poor"), or do they inspire believers to alleviate the contemporary Passion of our world? Images of Mary elevate the Virgin as unique among women, sometimes portraying her as other-worldly and idealized. Do they *numb* us or *sensitize* us to the plight of real, ordinary women who suffer? As one feminist theologian wrote, Mary herself is in need of liberation. How can we give her a voice—without cheapening her silence? How can we honor her stalwart vigil—without becoming passive ourselves?

For the short space of not even three full days (lowered late on Wednesday of Holy Week in preparation for the *Triduum*, raised back to her pedestal in festive robes on Saturday), the Virgin of Solitude comes closer. Her nearness quivers like a compass.

She teaches me about the mystery of suffering. To bear it fully without being defeated by it. To confront evil, even if this means simply not closing my eyes, keeping gaze fixed when words fail. Not accepting or resigning myself to suffering, and never laying down the task of witness. Co-sufferer with humanity, like her son, the Virgin is an advocate for the fullness of life. She willingly risks the consequences her commitment might entail. Even in her silent stance, she defies evil. She stands there pointing the way into eternity, hands "like lilies" clinging to hope, the very face of courage in suffering.

Hers is the waiting in expectancy while experiencing the dark night of the soul—an awful parallel to her anticipation during pregnancy. As once she traveled "in haste" to the hill country with the news of a miraculous conception, after another long journey this same village woman—now a bent widow—bears the message that again she is about to become a mother. In her posture of grief, for the second time she faces the pain of labor, and, instead of cowering, she leans into it as the waves of suffering flood her body. In it, she meets her own desire: to be swept up in the embrace of a fierce and tender God, who sends us forth to bring that same embrace we long for to others.

Witnessing the loss of her son, she does not close her eyes to any of it. She weeps for him while inheriting the children of the future, her son incarnated again and again in the persons of those who suffer throughout history. The gateway to his life, she now ministers as midwife to his death, standing by as his precious life's energy wanes, drop by drop, breath by breath. She *must* be there, she does not want to be there, but this is the task that has been given to her, and she accepts it. She does not accept the murder of her son and she definitely would not have chosen it, but she will not relinquish what must come: the next present moment of standing there and just being alive—even though every fiber in her body wishes she could die. She will *not* close her eyes, she will *not* avert her gaze, because she hears his voice in utter abandonment call out the first line of Psalm 22, "My God, my God, why have you forsaken me?" and she has no words of consolation for him. No words exist that can assuage his agony. Yet, even if all she can give him is her silence, she will offer it freely, and she will not abandon him nor move away in case he should have sudden need of her gaze.

Whether one cries or stands dry-eyed, whether one rages or remains wordless, the important thing is to keep one's eyes open, gaze fixed, even though the heart is desperate to look away, knees and strength failing. Memory remains, a stubborn refuge, its echoes reverberating through history in a multitude of crosses strung through the centuries; the trains to Auschwitz, the Middle Passage, the Trail of Tears, the shameful legacy of every man and every woman—each one the child of a *mater dolorosa*—forced to carry a cross.

Since getting to know the Virgin of Solitude, glimpsing who she *really* is, I have started seeing *madres dolorosas* everywhere. Some speak to me of the stuff of daily tragedies: a widow with eleven children living in a hillside shack; a migrant with a severely disabled child. Others have stories of more epic proportions: the wives of the protestors killed in the movement; the mother of the graduate student, waiting for her daughter's return from prison.

I have come across contemporary artists and writers who compare the *Mater Dolorosa* to mothers of war victims everywhere, especially those who have lost a son or daughter in Iraq. Others see in the figure of the sorrowful Virgin the veiled women of the Middle East, where bloodshed seems never-ending. And in a metaphor I find provocative, the lyrics to one song name her as the earth itself, a great *Mater Dolorosa* suffering *for* us and suffering *because of* us.

Historically, this Oaxacan virgin has been defined by men in varying positions of ecclesial power (Bohórquez, Morelos, Gillow). But ultimately, the *Mater Dolorosa* is symbolically feminine, putting Christians in touch with Nature's transformative processes of birth, menstruation, death. Representing the third stage of every woman's cycle—bereft, aging, reflective—she is the wise woman who anchors our lives. In this triad, the diminutive, inviolate Juquilita is cast as Maiden; the all-embracing Guadalupana takes center stage as Universal Mother; and the Soledad appears as mysteriously regenerating Crone. Beautiful because of—not in spite of—her age, she welcomes us at the final threshold through which we must all pass.

Like the figure of Mary in the gospels, the Virgin of Solitude plays a definite role, that of the Great Signifier. Each evangelist gives us a different version, but in all of them Mary of Nazareth leads us to her Son. (Even John, who does not give the Mother of Jesus a name, places her clearly at the beginning and end of the seven signs that frame his gospel.) The Star of the Sea, *Stella Maris*, Mary shows the way. In her guiding figure, we find clues for our own journeys.

For the Virgin of Soledad is the Virgin of Juquila who is the Virgin of Guadalupe. The *Mater Dolorosa* waits in eternal receptive patience, but she is only *one* image of Mary—the same unwed pregnant teenager who sang the Magnificat; the same refugee mother who crossed a border into exile.

The Virgin of Solitude remains perpetually affixed to the foot of the cross, as if herself nailed to the scene. However, Mary of Nazareth is, at heart, a traveler. She comes down from her pedestal and joins us on our life journeys—collective and individual. Every step is weighted by a cross, every pilgrimage opens a path. A woman fully human and fully alive has gone before us, a disciple in search of the Reign of God. Her courage makes contemporary believers sing:

> As you walk the roads of life
> Often far from home
> With you travels Mary:
> You are never alone.
>
> Mary, come walk with us
> Mary, come walk with us.
>
> Though people you meet
> May walk unawares

Never hold back your hand
From reaching for theirs.

People will tell you
Nothing can change.
Fight for a new world
Fight for truth, anyway.

Even though your steps
Seem taken in vain,
You open new paths:
Others will follow the same.[28]

V

¿Quien es esa estrella
Que a los hombres guía?
La Reina del cielo
La Virgen Maria.

Caminen, hermanos
Por esa vereda
Y vamos gustosos
Siguiendo la estrella.

También a los magos
Los guiaba una estrella
Y hallaron gozosos
A la virgen bella.

La Virgen les muestra
Al niño Jesús,
El que ha de salvarnos
Clavado en la cruz.

Que alegría me causa,
Señora, este día
Saber que caminas
En mi compañía.

Si somos tus hijos
Tú eres nuestra madre
Míranos Señora,
No nos desampares.

Who is that star,
Which guides so many?
The Queen of Heaven,
The Virgin Mary.

Let us walk, all of us
On that path so far
As joyfully we journey
To follow the star.

The Wise Men also
Followed a star's light
And found the Virgin
In joy and delight.

The Virgin reveals
Her Child, the Christ
He who must save us
On a cross crucified.

How happy I am,
Today, my Lady
Knowing that you walk
In my company.

If we are your children
Then our Mother you
    must be.
Look upon us, do not
    disown us
Dearest Lady.

Angélicas tropas	Heavenly troops,
Salid al encuentro	Go forth to meet her
Que allí los espera	She waits for you,
La Madre del Verbo.	Mother of the Word.
¡Que Virgen tan pura!	The purest Virgin,
¡Que Madre tan bella!	Mother most beautiful, by far!
Y yo les pregunto,	I ask you again,
¿Quien es esa estrella?	Who is that star?
Nosotros cantando	Singing, singing
Seguimos su huella	We walk in her footsteps
Y al cielo entraremos	And someday will join her
A vivir con ella.	On heaven's doorstep.

EPILOGUE

✶ ✶ ✶ ✶ ✶ ✶

Every summer, my brother and I went to visit my grandmother in what used to be rural Ohio. We traveled to her dusty old house filled with madonnas in a small town surrounded by vast tracts of grape arbors. Summers were hot and hazy, and the heat—combined with the humidity of the Black River that flowed through the backyard—kept the house at an uncomfortable temperature, even at night. As a child, to escape the heat of my attic bedroom, I would crawl into my grandmother's bed. Next to the comforting soft pillow of her body, I felt her gentleness envelop me like a mantle, the scapulars she habitually wore sticking lightly to my damp skin. The lull of the boxy radio next to her bed and the drone of her reciting the rosary sank into my ears as I drifted into dreams.

When my grandmother died, I jealously laid claim to her nightgowns and to the scapulars, to the tattered holy cards I could not bear to throw away. Still scented with talcum powder, the nightgowns of satin-like polyester or worn cotton with their wide bands of lace had been discolored to ivory from decades of wear. The scapulars were so frayed that most stared back at me like blank faces sewn on patches of sturdy brown felt, stubborn cords holding together the two white swatches.

Only one scapular, protected by a coating of plastic, preserves a distinct image, that of the Virgin of Carmel holding the Christ Child. The words "My Mother, My Confidence" are printed on the back. Both mother and child look out, head on, toward the viewer. They appear intensely interested in whatever they are seeing, projecting a sense of calm and compassion with no trace whatsoever of frivolity or foreboding.

This emblem has become more and more meaningful to me over time. The brown-haired Virgin holds her head up, conveying an air of

175

grace and decision. Her face is turned slightly toward her son, while she simultaneously shares her attention with the viewer. The closeness of the Christ child's curls to his Mother's veiled head lends the pose a sense of unity and tenderness. Their joined gaze, relentlessly projected outward, firmly takes the world—with all its beauty and fragility—into view.

Although I have moved beyond the images of the Virgin Mary that I inherited, I have not left all of them behind. This one remains in its place of honor, my psalter (which has journeyed on all my travels). The image from the tattered remnant of a scapular is one-dimensional, flat and colorless. It is old-fashioned—belonging to the spirituality of a world that is other, that is not my own—and it dates from a time before I was born, arising from a style of devotion that I will never know.

But this picture, retrieved from my grandmother's trove of religious paraphernalia, propelled my search for contemporary expressions of devotion. It belongs among the many faces of the Virgin Mary, precisely because the Mother of God wears different faces.

Mary safeguards Jesus' humanity by entering into the mystery of his Incarnation, taking on semblances from each of Christianity's multiple cultures. She reminds us, as do the Resurrection accounts, that Christ can be found among "the living" (Luke 24:5).

The Virgin Mary, herself, is alive and present among us.

I have watched young people by the hundreds make the arduous pilgrimage—on foot or by bicycle—through Oaxaca's most treacherous mountains. Their prize? The reward of gazing upon the Virgin's face and standing for one perfect moment under her dusty mantle.

I have seen a Mexican Madonna in the corn camps and apple orchards of New York, illumined by the torch that lights the way for a new generation of Christians in the United States. The Virgin of Guadalupe appears once more to the Juan Diegos whom she chooses to bear her message.

I have witnessed *her* witnessing *for us* as she stands at the foot of her Son's cross in Oaxaca, and I have gazed upon her face as she—*still*—gazes upon His.

My grandmother's scapular helped to propel my search for more meaningful contemporary images of the Virgin Mary, but my encounter with *other* representations ultimately brought my attention back to this one with newly appreciative eyes. The very experience of encountering her in places far from home seemed to deepen my relationship with the Mother of God, allowing me to return to my inherited images with an altered view. It is as if *my* crossing borders allowed me to enter more deeply into *her* mystery, the mystery of Mary as woman and as symbol.

Again I am struck by how Marian devotion over the centuries has affirmed her ability to traverse thresholds of time and geography, crossing over again and again. Seeking the same relevance and fervor of devotion that my grandmother found, I now saw in her favorite images representations that open paths toward a relationship with the Mother of God: pilgrimage routes to be traveled.

Isn't it surprising that a woman about whom so little is known historically has inspired an infinite and immense tide in the human imagination, like a "sea that no one exhausts"?

I had been looking for a literal interpretation when I should have been seeking a symbolic one—one that could have practical applications in my own life. I had thirsted for images of Mary that would empower me as a woman. Instead, I found a source of strength in my own engagement with these images. Rather than discovering a scriptural passage that fashions Mary as a twenty-first century woman, or finding *the* perfect representation to satisfy my requisites for a politically-correct madonna, I met her in ongoing encounters of mutual discovery. Neither an intriguing idol nor a revolutionary roadmap, the Virgin Mary offers Christians something quite simple: her self. Mary is, first and foremost, a saint with whom Christians have a relationship: a mother. Her blessing carries us over the borders of our lives.

✱   ✱   ✱   ✱   ✱

At the end of the three years that my husband and I spent as foreign missioners in Oaxaca, we prepared to return to our ministry with migrants and immigrants in New York. During the farewell gathering held by my base ecclesial community, one of its members, a Mixtec single mother who had emigrated from a village to live in one of the capital's shantytowns, made a proposal. She suggested that they give us *la bendición* (traditional blessing), "like we do in our villages when our people go north."

Members of the group lined up one by one to trace the sign of the cross over us. My children's wondering faces showed that they did not understand everything, but even the twins, who by then were toddlers, knew that something momentous was happening.

Before long into the short ceremony, every adult present had begun to weep. I knew intuitively that the tears our friends shed were not only for us, but also for the family members and fellow villagers who had gone to the other side, *el otro lado*, of the border. *My* tears, of course, were for them—bound to Oaxaca's uncertain fate.

The Virgin Mary plays this same role for generation upon generation of believers. Casting her famous mantle over her children, she blesses us on our journeys—whatever route they take, wherever they might lead.

Each of these three Mexican representations—the Virgin of Juquila, the Virgin of Guadalupe, and the Virgin of Solitude—rooted as they are in particular cultural expressions, illustrates with singular precision a portrait that is unmistakably recognizable. Devotees know them as different images of the same Mother of God. In glimpsing her face—already turned toward ours—we see her; and in reflecting upon her face (like a nursing infant attuned to a mother's gaze), we also know ourselves. Our true identity is revealed: we are children of God's own mother.

During that blessing, I knew with confidence that even as we were about to travel north, in some irrevocable way, we had been indelibly changed. I had crossed over.

VI

Adiós, Reina del Cielo,	Farewell, Queen of Heaven
Madre del Salvador	Mother of the Savior
Adiós ¡oh Madre mía!	Farewell, my own Mother!
Adiós, adiós, adiós.	Farewell, farewell, farewell.

De tu divino rostro	I leave with regret
Me alejo con pesar	Your face so sweet
Permíteme que vuelva	Allow me to return someday
Tus plantas a besar.	To your holy feet.

Al dejarte, ¡oh María!	Hearts weeps when they
No acierta el corazón,	Say good-bye to you, O Mary
Te lo entrego Señora,	Take mine with you
Dame tu bendición.	Give me your blessing, O Lady.

Adiós, Hija del Padre,	Farewell, Daughter of the Father
Madre del Hijo, adiós.	Mother of the Son, farewell
¡Adiós ¡oh Madre mía!	Farewell, my own Mother
¡Oh, casta esposa, adiós!	Chaste Spouse of the Spirit, farewell.

Adiós oh, Madre Virgen,	Farewell, Virgin Mother
Más pura que la luz;	Pure as radiant Light
Jamás, jamás me olvides	Remember me always
Delante de Jesús.	Before your Son, the Christ.

NOTES

1. My Mother, My Confidence

1. See Jaroslov Pelikan, *Mary Through the Centuries* (New York: Yale University Press, 1996), 57.

2. Toribio Tapia Bahena, Fourth Mexican Workshop on Migrant Ministry, Oaxaca, 2005.

3. Latina and Latin American feminists have exposed the ambiguities of the maternal role, which must be reformed precisely *because of* its vast potential for damaging or for empowering both women and men.

4. The closest term I can think of in English, *head of household*, primarily lends an economic connotation, while *padres de familia* carries civic and moral connotations.

5. Jeanette Rodriguez, *Our Lady of Guadalupe: Faith and Empowerment among Mexican-American Women* (Austin, TX: University of Texas Press, 1994), 163.

6. By Alyshia Gálvez (New York: New York University Press, 2009).

7. These early interactions extend into speech acquisition; the ability to feel empathy for others; individual skills and talents; and the development of personality. Allan N. Schore, PhD, "The Neurobiology of Attachment and Early Personality Organization" in the *Journal of Prenatal and Perinatal Psychology and Health* 16, no. 3 (Spring, 2002). Schore writes, "To be a biological human and to be a psychological human are two very different things. To have the body of a human being is one thing, but to be able to feel that one's needs are of value to self and others, to have a secure personality, only emerges as a result of having the experience, at the very beginning of life, of being part of an ongoing relationship . . . with an emotionally attuned adult human, a 'good-enough' mother."

8. This dogma is often confused with the virgin birth. The Immaculate Conception refers to the Church teaching that Mary from the moment of her conception was untainted by original sin—a topic hotly debated in the Middle Ages.

9. Chapter 22 of the *Sindicato Nacional de Trabajadores de Educación*, National Educational Workers' Union. See my articles in *The National*

Catholic Reporter, October 13, 2006, October 20, 2006, and December 15, 2006; the *Catholic Agitator,* November 2006; and the *Catholic Worker,* December 2006.

10. Most human rights groups—including Amnesty International—have estimated the number of deaths *directly caused* by the conflict at between twenty and twenty-three. Many other deaths were indirectly related to the conflict. I translated testimonies of the widows of José Jiménez Colmenares, Lorenzo San Pablo Cervantes, and Pánfilo Hernández Vásquez.

11. *María sigue acompañando a su Hijo que vive y sufre con nosotros. Ella está cuando luchamos cada día para que a nuestra familia no le falte el pan, el agua, la vivienda, la educación, la fe... María nos acompaña cuando unidos buscamos que no nos falte lo necesario para vivir con dignidad de personas. María da fuerza a tantas madres que por un pedazo de pan pasan su vida lavando ropa ajena, vendiendo, trabajando en el campo o en las maquiladoras con un salario de miseria... Da fuerza a tantas madres que sufren el dolor de ver asesinados injustamente a sus hijos; está presente junto a las madres que exigen la presencia de hermanos o hijos desaparecidos por gobiernos injustos. Virgen María, Madre de Jesús y Madre nuestra, danos la fuerza para seguir tu ejemplo. Ayúdanos a transformar el dolor de tantas madres en un deseo muy grande de trabajar para que en nuestras familias y comunidades los hijos puedan crecer en un ambiente de paz, justicia y amor.*

2. On the Road to Juquila

1. Historically Oaxaca consists of La Canada, La Mixteca, La Costa, Popoaloapan, the Isthmus of Tehuantepec, Valles Centrales and Sierras; now, the Sierra is divided into Sierra Norte and Sierra Sur.

2. Victor Turner and Edith L. B. Turner, *Image and Pilgrimage in Christian Culture* (New York: Columbia University Press, 1978).

3. Ibid., 32.

4. See Mariana Martinez, "Bike-Riding Faith: Devotion for the Juquila Virgin" in *La Prensa San Diego,* January 10, 2003, for a journalist's account of bicycle pilgrimage.

5. Turner and Turner, *Image and Pilgrimage in Christian Culture,* 14.

6. Juan Castro Méndez, *La Virgen de Juquila en la Historia, Oraciones, Alabanzas y Poemas,* Secretaria de Educación Pública, 2000, 03-2000-021011462700-01, Instituto Nacional del Derecho del Autor.

7. Turner and Turner, *Image and Pilgrimage in Christian Culture,* 6.

8. A topic for speculation is whether without the Virgin Mary, evangelization —whether in the Americas or anywhere else in the non-Christian world— would have been even remotely possible.

9. Danica Coto, February 28, 2006, *The Charlotte Observer.*

10. Anthropologists have proposed an alternate translation, "people of the words that work."

11. *"Las montanas de Oaxaca fueron refugio para quienes no aceptaron la imposición del nuevo régimen."* Margarita Dalton, *Breve Historia de Oaxaca* (México: El Colegio de México, Fideicomiso Historia de las Americas, Fondo de Cultura Económica, 2004), 84.

12. Tomás Cruz Lorenzo, "Aspectos de la Religiosidad Chatina," in *Pueblos Indígenas de Oaxaca*, ed. Alicia Mabel Barabas, Miguel Alberto Bartolomé, and Benjamín Maldonado (Oaxaca: Instituto Nacional de Antropología e Historia, Fondo de Cultura Económica, Gobierno del Estado de Oaxaca/Secretaria de Asuntos Indígenas, 2003), 73. Alicia Barabas, in this anthology and in other works, has written compellingly about the Chatino nation, ethnicity in Oaxaca, and even Zapotec Marian apparitions.

13. Robert Ricard, *The Spiritual Conquest of Mexico*, trans. Lesley Byrd Simpson (Berkeley: University of California Press, 1966), 187.

14. Turner and Turner, *Image and Pilgrimage in Christian Culture.*

15. A European phenomenon, Black Virgins are images that corroded in the soil after they had been buried for protection from iconoclasts or Islamic intruders; blackened by centuries of candles and incense; or intentionally painted or carved from dark-grained wood. Famous Black Madonnas include the Virgin of Monserrat, the Virgin of Czestokova, and the Spanish Virgin of Guadalupe. See China Galland's *Longing for Darkness* (New York: Viking Penguin, 1990).

16. Turner and Turner, *Image and Pilgrimage in Christian Culture*, 28.

17. According to one story, the Viking raider Rolf Ganger was deterred from sacking the original Chartres Cathedral by the sight of the *Sancta Camisia* displayed by the archbishop (the *camisia*, said to have been worn by Mary, is still venerated at present-day Chartres). A town in Italy, Prato, even today displays a green strip of wool—Mary's sash—for veneration five times a year; the Syrian Orthodox Church also claims to own the exact same relic, housed in what is known as "the Church of the Virgin of the Girdle" in Homs.

18. *"Dulce Madre, no te alejes, ven conmigo a todas partes y nunca solo/a me dejes. Ya que nos proteges tanto como verdadera Madre, cúbrenos con tu manto y haz que nos bendiga el Padre, el Hijo y el Espíritu Santo."*

19. *"Madre querida, Virgen de Juquila, Virgen de nuestra esperanza, tuya es nuestra vida. Cuídanos de todo mal. Si en este mundo de injusticias, miseria y pecado, si ves que nuestra vida se turba, no nos abandones, Madre querida. Protege a los peregrinos, acompáñanos por todos los caminos. Vela por los pobres sin sustento y el pan que se les quita, retribúyeselos. Acompáñanos en toda nuestra vida y líbranos de todo tipo de pecado."*

20. Rosaurora Espinoza.

21. Figures from the United Nations Population Fund.

22. Figures from the American Civil Liberties Union.

3. The Mother's Gaze

1. For contemporary Guadalupan theology, see Virgilio Elizondo's *Guadalupe: Mother of the New Creation* (Maryknoll, NY: Orbis Books, 1997); Jeanette Rodriguez's *Our Lady of Guadalupe: Faith and Empowerment among Mexican-American Women* (Texas: University of Texas Press, 1994); and Carl Anderson and Eduardo Chávez's *Our Lady of Guadalupe: Mother of the Civilization of Love* (New York: Doubleday, 2009).

2. In 1531—the year in which tradition sets the apparitions—Zumárraga was the bishop-elect.

3. Richard Kuhn, who went on to win the Nobel Prize for chemistry in 1938, made the finding in 1936 that the original pigments used to paint the *tilma* are not from a known vegetable, mineral, or animal source.

4. Philip Serna Callahan carried out this study in 1979.

5. See the official Basilica website for the various investigations conducted on the mystery of the Virgin's eyes.

6. Leoncio Garza Valdés was engaged by prelates of the Basilica and Mexican episcopacy to study the *tilma*.

7. The term "Aztec"—mistakenly used as a blanket term to refer to the indigenous nations of Mexico—designates a political conglomerate of three ethnic groups, the dominant of which at the time of the Conquest was the Mexica, who belonged to the wider Nahuatl-speaking populations of Central Mexico.

8. Elizondo introduced *mestizaje* as a theological concept in his groundbreaking *Galilean Journey: The Mexican-American Promise* (Maryknoll, NY: Orbis Books, 1983).

9. Leaders from our parish's other Latin American countries of origin, for example, complain that they are summarily referred to as "Mexican"; another common mistaken designation in New York labels all Spanish *speakers* "Spanish."

10. Constantine Cavarnos, *Orthodox Iconography* (Belmont, MA: The Institute for Byzantine and Modern Greek Studies, Inc., 1977), 31–32.

11. Stafford Poole, CM, *Our Lady of Guadalupe: The Origins and Sources of a Mexican National Symbol, 1531–1797* (Tucson, AZ: The University of Arizona Press, 1997).

12. The possibility, included in Poole's book, that Nahua Christians may have coined this term as their own name for the Virgin Mary should not be discounted; the designation affirms, rather than negates, the citation by Bernardino de Sahagún of Tepeyac as an indigenous pilgrimage center honoring a native mother goddess. This symbolism acquired a distinctly Christian character after the Conquest.

13. In an ancient native tradition, the twin of Quetzalcoatl, when entrusted with a message for the human world, would assume the shape of a dog and run with a lit torch in its mouth.

14. Joel Magellan Reyes has since left the Jesuit Order. The Tepeyac Association now functions as an independent organization.

15. Documented and undocumented nationals of an estimated seventy-nine countries died in the terrorist attack.

16. *"Mensajeros por la dignidad de un pueblo dividido por la frontera."*

17. *"[Esta es la] primera vez que la Carrera [fue] muy bien recibida en la Ciudad de Nueva York."*

18. The Cristero Rebellion (1926–1929) was an outcry against Mexican presidents' efforts to replace the Roman Catholic Church with a national one controlled by the federal government.

19. Mariano Cuevas, SJ, found fragments of a copy of *Inin huey tlamahuicoltzin* ("This is the great miracle") known commonly as the *Relación Primitiva*, which at one time belonged to the Jesuits.

20. Robert Ricard wrote, "It was born, and it matured and triumphed, under the active influence of the episcopate . . . in the midst of Dominican and Augustinian indifference, and despite the hostile anxiety of the Franciscans"; see *The Spiritual Conquest of Mexico*, trans. Lesley Byrd Simpson (Berkeley: University of California Press, 1966), 144. Stafford Poole casts a more scouring light on the two bishops. Zumárraga's prolific records tell nothing of the apparitions (Poole dismisses apologetic explanations of a paper shortage during colonial times). While Zumárraga's successor advocated the devotion, he fell far short of granting the prestige we take for granted: during Alonso de Montúfar's episcopate, a small structure (known to have existed since 1555) received devotees; only in 1609 was a building of solid masonry constructed.

21. Cuauhtlatoatzin, given the baptismal name Juan Diego, was married to a woman whose Christian name is recorded as Maria Lucia. Apparently, she died before her husband (accounts differ as to whether this was before or after the apparitions). Local traditions tended to attribute a state of continence to their marriage, although testimonies indicate that the couple had at least one son. According to tradition he died in 1548, the same year Zumárraga died. Each year in Mexico, a huge clan gathers in a family reunion as Juan Diego's descendants.

22. *"Muchos indios se ahorcan, otros se dejan morir de hambre, otros se envenenan con hierbas; hay madres que matan a los hijos que acaban de dar a luz, y dicen que lo hacen para ahorrarles los sufrimientos que ellas pasan."* A missive from the Spanish Crown to the colonial authorities of the province of Guatemala called for humane treatment of the native population, citing these examples. Real Cédula de 27 mayo 1582.

23. Since the time this mission started, two parishes in the area began having a weekly Spanish Mass, and pastoral projects for Latinos are slowly gaining increased support.

24. *Bendito, bendito, bendito, sea Dios*
    los ángeles cantan y alaban a Dios.
    Yo creo, Jesús Mío, que estas en el altar
    oculto en la hostia, te vengo a adorar.

25. *Hemos venido a este lugar para adorar al Señor*
    Hemos venido a este lugar para adorar al Señor
    Yo te agradezco
    por todo lo que has hecho
    todo lo que haces
    y todo lo que harás.

26. Each of these adaptations begins the Hail Mary with a title corresponding to Mary's relationships to the three persons of the Trinity and proclaims
her respectively virgin before, during, and after Jesus' birth.

4. Her Silence, Our Song

1. *"María Santísima de la Soledad al Pie de la Cruz."* Variations of the no-
longer existent sign read, *"Nuestra Señora de la Soledad al pie de la cruz"* (Our
Lady of Solitude at the foot of the cross) or *"La Santísima Madre de la Soledad
al pie de la cruz"* (The Most Holy Mother of Solitude at the foot of the cross).

2. Everardo Ramírez Bohórquez, *Oaxaca en la Soledad* (Oaxaca: Carte-
les Editores, 2000).

3. An exact figure cannot be determined, but attempts at demographic
reconstruction estimate the native population of the state to have been somewhere between 1.5 and 2.5 million in 1521.

4. At the time of the Conquest, European medicine also routinely practiced bloodletting. On another note—the atrocities committed by the European invaders at times rivaled human sacrifice for their brutality. See Eduardo
Galeano's *The Open Veins of Latin America* (New York: Monthly Review
Press, 1973) and his trilogy *Memory of Fire* (New York: Pantheon Books,
1985), both translated by Cedric Belfrage.

5. *Los Negritos, El Tigre, La Danza de la Pluma, Los Santiagüitos, La
Danza de los Machetes, El Jarabe Mixteco, Los Centeños, Las Chilenas, Los Sones
Costeños* and *El Fandango del Valle.*

6. *"¡No sois vos, Señora, la Virgen de la Soledad!"*

7. *"... los arcos atrevidos, las bóvedas soberbias, la finura de los detalles, así como la
grandiosidad del pensamiento que se manifiesta en el conjunto."* José Antonio Gay,
Historias de Oaxaca (Imprenta del Comercio de Dublán y Cia., 1881).

8. See, especially, chapters on this subject in Marina Warner's *Alone of
All Her Sex* (New York: Vintage Books [Random House], 1976) and
Jaroslav Pelikan's *Mary through the Centuries* (New York: Yale University
Press, 1996).

9. The Seven Sorrows of Mary are the prophecy of Simeon (Luke 2:34–35); the flight into Egypt (Matthew 2:13–14); the loss of Jesus in the temple (Luke 2:43); Mary meeting Jesus as he carries his cross (inferred from Luke 23:26–27); Mary at the foot of the cross (John 19:25–27a); Mary receiving Jesus' body (inferred from Mark 15, 46–47 and John 19:40–42); and the burial of Jesus (from the same texts in Mark and John).

10. See Elizabeth A. Johnson's *Truly Our Sister: A Theology of Mary in the Communion of Saints* (New York: Continuum, 2003).

11. The *Stabat Mater* has been attributed to Pope John XXII (d. 1334), Pope Innocent III (d. 1216), Bonaventure (d. 1274), Gregory the Great (d. 604), and Bernard of Clairveaux (d. 1153). Tradition generally favors authorship by Franciscan Jacopone da Todi, although historians dispute this attribution.

12. Warner, *Alone of All Her Sex*, 262.

13. In Oaxaca's central valleys, this practice has been eclipsed by the identical tradition of giving out drinks, popsicles, and so forth on the Day of the Samaritan Woman, which takes place during Lent and coincides with the lectionary cycle reading from John's Gospel (4:1–42).

14. A Spanish translation from the Latin:

Estaba la Madre dolorosa
junto a la Cruz, llorosa
en que pendía su Hijo.

Su alma gimiente,
contristada y doliente
atravesó la espada.

¡O cuán triste y afligida
estuvo aquella bendita
Madre del Unigénito!

Languidecía y se dolía
la piadosa Madre que veía
las penas de su excelso Hijo.

¿Qué hombre no lloraría
si a la madre de Cristo viera
en tanto suplicio?

¿Quién no se entristecería
a la Madre contemplando
con su doliente Hijo?

Por los pecados de su gente
vio a Jesús en los tormentos
y doblegado por los azotes.

Vio a su dulce Hijo
muriendo desolado
al entregar su espíritu.

Ea, Madre, fuente de amor
hazme sentir tu dolor
contigo quiero llorar.

Haz que mi corazón arda
en el amor de mi Dios
y en cumplir su voluntad.

Santa Madre, yo te ruego
que me traspases las llagas
del Crucificado en el corazón.

De tu Hijo malherido
que por mí tanto sufrió
reparte conmigo las penas.

Déjame llorar contigo
condolerme por tu Hijo
mientras yo esté vivo.

Junto a la Cruz contigo estar
y contigo asociarme
en el llanto es mi deseo.

Virgen de Vírgenes preclara
no te amargues ya conmigo
déjame llorar contigo.

Haz que llore la muerte de Cristo
hazme socio de su pasión
haz que me quede con sus llagas.

Haz que me hieran sus llagas
haz que con la Cruz me embriague
y con la Sangre de tu Hijo.

Para que no me queme en las llamas
defiéndeme tú, Virgen santa
en el día del juicio.

Cuando, Cristo, haya de irme
concédeme que tu Madre me guíe
a la palma de la victoria.

Y cuando mi cuerpo muera
haz que a mi alma se conceda
del Paraíso la gloria. Amén.

15. See Judges 13:2–5; 1 Samuel 1:1–20; Luke 1:5–17.

16. Jon Sobrino, *Jesus the Liberator: A Historical-Theological View* (Maryknoll, NY: Orbis Books, 2004), 246.

17. In 1900, Oaxaca's inhabitants numbered 948,633, and by 1910, 1,040,398.

18. Ironically, under Mexico's single-party system it was easier to impeach politicians or force their resignations; now, competing political parties have more at stake and keep their members in office.

19. Ramírez Bohórquez, *Oaxaca en la Soledad*, 27.

20. *"Fiesta grande fue para el pueblo oaxaqueño, que una vez más mostró su unidad en señal de reverencia y amor a la Virgen Patrona, patrona igualmente de los marineros que suelen traerle perlas del más raro oriente."* Ramírez Bohórquez, *Oaxaca en la Soledad*, 30.

21. *"Es que, además de la profanación, por todos execrada, se ha perdido una joya de inestimable precio porque en ella se fundieron la amorosa tradición conservada y acrecentada a lo largo de tres y medio siglos..."* Ibid, p. 36.

22. The state population grew from 1,727,266 in 1960 to 2,686,968 in 1990. The staggering trend of growth has continued, and in 2007 the state population numbered 3.2 million.

23. The egregiously unsatisfactory investigation of the theft carried out by the state Justice Department led many frustrated Oaxacans to speculate that state politicians had stalled the investigation in an attempt to deflate Carrasco's popularity.

24. The archbishop's offer to provide mediation was turned down by the coalition of the teachers' union and the popular movement. Nevertheless, on several occasions, he acted behind the scenes to arrange negotiations between the coalition and Mexico's Interior Secretary.

25. Movement protestors claimed that at least one child had been killed on June 14. An exhaustive human rights report by archdiocesan priest José Rentería compiled from scores of interviews details numerous human rights abuses committed on that day but does not support this rumor.

26. Governor Ulises Ruíz Ortiz admitted that approximately 80 percent of the 215 people detained on November 25 and 26, 2006, were arrested unjustly; in the most egregious instances, pedestrians who had had nothing to do with the march were randomly picked up by police and even tortured.

27. A tactic used in Central America's civil wars and in Oaxaca's neighbor state, Guerrero, during the 1970s.

28. *Mientras recorres la vida*
Tú nunca solo estás
Contigo por el camino
Santa María va.

Ven con nosotros al caminar, Santa María ven
Ven con nosotros al caminar, Santa María ven.

Si por el mundo los hombres
Sin conocerse van
Nunca niegues tu mano
Al que contigo está.

Aunque te dicen algunos
Que nada puede cambiar
Lucha por un mundo nuevo
Lucha por la verdad.

Aunque parezcan tus pasos
Inútil caminar
Tú vas abriendo caminos
Otros los seguirán.